Pregnant with a Seed

Georgetta Ward

ISBN:
ISBN-13:

<u>**Dedication**</u>

I would love to tell the Lord, Thank you, for inspiring me to write this book and its content.

This book is dedicated to my family, my husband, Bishop Ralph Peter Ward III, my three wonderful children, Chastity Ward, Elijah Walls, and Ashley Walls. I also would like to Thank Lamar Hargrove for tirelessly typing, both him and my eldest daughter Chastity. I would like to thank my mom for all the wisdom and knowledge passed on. Love you all

God has sent me into your life to be your support person. Push, woman of God....PUSH!

This book is for those who have been impregnated with the word of God and delivery has yet to come. Push your seed.

-Thanks.

- Lady Georgetta Ward

<u>**INTRODUCTION**</u>

I remember pushing and being in such great pain. That particular type of pain was one that I had never experienced before in my life. I was trying to give birth to my daughter (Chastity). I remember screaming, crying, being weary, yelling, feeling helplessness and finally exhaustion. There were so many different people that came to my room, and I remember squeezing their hands so hard for comfort and strength because it was not time for me to push yet. I knew that I needed help in overcoming this delivery (I couldn't do it alone). I can remember the nurse coming into my room because I was in so much pain. I thought she came to help me, but instead she began saying, "it can't be that bad; you have been given the epidural pain medication and it should be working by now, your body should be numb." I could not receive what the nurse was saying, because I was feeling the contractions, my water had already broken, it was time for me to deliver and I was in a place where my seed was on the inside fully developed and ready to manifest, I could not muster up enough strength to push it out.

<u>Some of your right now, God has planted his seed on the inside; He has equipped you and given you directions. He has given you the tools you need to deliver.</u>

The nurse that was assigned to me had begun to get frustrated with me because I could not deliver. She made it noticeable by her vocal tone. She just could not believe that I was unable to push out my seed.

There are other people who can see your purpose and plan, and have no idea that you are struggling with who you are and what seed has been placed on the inside of you, and how to produce it. Everyone else can see it, and believe that you can push it out (people are waiting on you to deliver). However, there you are trying to push, but have not yet begun dilating. Your cervix will not open and your seed is dying on the inside of you. I kept telling the nurse that I was not feeling the medicine, I was not numb and I could feel the pains. Nothing was putting my body at ease. Therefore, the nurse left the room, frustrated at me. A few moments later she returned checking the IV cord, my pulse, my heart rate, and blood pressure finding nothing out of order. She checked to see if I had a fever and did an ultrasound to see if something was going wrong; they were normal too. This left everything up to me to deliver. At this point (still in extreme pain) neither the nurse nor the doctor knew what was wrong, or what was causing my pains.

I began crying and calling on the name of the Lord. All of my family was there. There was another woman who started out with me and went into the delivery room and instantly gave birth and she was holding her seed. Here I was waiting, five hours, ten hours, and twelve hours had passed and I was in too much pain to push. My mother, who was my support person, came into my room. I began telling her about the unbearable pain that I was encountering so much so that it took my ability to push. I began feeling disappointed, with tears of failure, and exhaustion. I began telling my mother that the pains had not stopped and were intensifying. As my mother watched tears roll down my face, I began calling on the name of Jesus. My mother prayed until the Holy Spirit began speaking, directing her to move the IV stand back, and look down at the socket. There I was for thirteen hours in extreme pain, when all I had to do was call on the name of Jesus and ask him to reveal the problem. God instantly revealed the problem to my support person, my mother, what was the source of all my pains and inability to push. The problem was that the IV machine was not plugged into the outlet, and therefore, I was not receiving the medicine that I needed to numb my body and soothe me. I was experiencing true child birth. There I was hooked up but not plugged in...

Woman of God, God has planted a seed into your life, and sometimes you are pushing all you know how. You are pushing from your spirit, your soul and yet it seems that your seed will not produce. You have been experiencing, pain, swelling, frustration, hurting, debt, toxic and weariness. You have suffered trying to deliver this seed and yet unsuccessful in your delivery.

I want to minister to your spirit and prophesy over your womb that your seed shall come forth, and it shall come forth with power, authority, and boldness (in the name of Jesus). Woman of God you have been experiencing let downs, and some knock downs too, but I want you to know that God is about to shake your womb, and allow every seed to come forth.

After sixteen hours it was time for delivery. After I searched and found my hindrances, I was able to deal with my situation.

Sometimes when you are in the delivery room, complications will occur. You may experience, pain, frustration, sweating and you may even begin to cry, but I encourage you to never stop pushing, push until something happens. Woman of God you're almost there, push woman of God! This is what you have been praying and fasting for, now P-U-S-H! Yes it is hard, it hurts, and it's difficult. Push out destiny, and push out your purpose. God gave you this assignment, and you will fulfill it. Push over the road blocks; push over obstacles, and over all handicaps. Push! , Your almost there. Push! Somebody is waiting on you for their deliverance, or for their breakthrough. Somebody is waiting for you to become their coach or support person. Why are you still in the delivery room? Why are you still unfruitful?

Table of Contents

CHAPTER 1

CONCEPTION

How do I know I've conceived?

<u>Conception: How do I know I've conceived?</u>

Sitting in our family home, in the living room, is what my family did to prepare for many family discussions. I can remember being sick, throwing up, feeling nauseated, fatigue, having mood swings, and other signs of pregnancy. I'll never forget how my "conception" was announced. My mother said "you're still not felling any better." I replied, "No." My younger brother yelled out, "Ain't nothing wrong with her but that she's pregnant," Pregnant, the word rung out over and over until it became painful to my ears.

My mother who was and still is a Pastor of a church, an anointed woman of God one who did not believe in premarital sex was also in the room.

I had just graduated from high school. I had all of these dreams, goals and ambitions in my life, my life was set however, trying to mix in with the wrong crowd, a crowd I certainly did not fit into or belong. I was in an unfamiliar circle going nowhere.

I was sick, throwing up, cramping and unsure of the changes that my body had been going through; I had taken cold and flu medicines and nothing would stop my symptoms. In the back of my mind, I knew I was pregnant, but I could not admit it from my lips. Sometimes you have to hear or have that feeling that God has planted a seed inside of you, unfortunately we can't easily admit it in our minds, and in our hearts, and our mouth cannot bring forth the words to speak it aloud. We find ourselves afraid, wondering what people would say or think about the conception. These feelings come whether you want them or not, whether you admit you are pregnant naturally or spiritually. There will always be critics who will try to make you place judgment upon others. That is why you cannot pattern your life after others and what their opinion of you is. Tell yourself right now I will not please others while being displeasing to myself. Someone is not going to like the decisions I make in life, but it will not be me. I'll use the words my sister, "Lisa" always says "They are not alpha neither are they omega" which means they are not the beginning nor the end. People have no heaven or hell to put you in. Stop living your life in the shadows of someone else.

Today start living for you!

As my brother shouted that out the room got very quiet and it seemed like everything started going in slow motion. I looked up and all eyes were on me. I quickly tried to defend myself, I shouted, "Boy you are so crazy!" However, my defense was overlooked and there I was trying to defend my pregnancy. Just like you, people can see the glory of God in you, they feel the anointing, they see the mantle, and they tell you, "Girl you are a Preacher" and because you don't see it right now or because it had not seem like you could carry God's Seed, you've begun denying what God is trying to deliver. I was the one that taught the young girls poise class; I was the one preaching God will keep you at a young age; I was telling them that if they slip, they should make sure they use condoms. I found myself doing the opposite in which I was telling others to do. In the midst of me lying, denying and making excuses, God allowed her to see right through me. It's something about denying that seed.

Just for a moment, look at Peter; he walked with the Lord and was one of God's chosen disciples. Peter was credited with being a leader of the twelve disciples. Jesus often singled Peter out for teaching intended for the entire group of disciples. Peter was the one who had loved Jesus. He would have done anything for Jesus, let him tell it. However; it was Peter (Luke 22:33) who said unto him, Lord I am ready to go with thee both into prison and to death. And Jesus said unto Peter, the rooster will not crow tomorrow morning until you have denied 3 times that you know me. While they were taking Jesus to the high priest's residence, there Peter was watching and following from afar. (Luke 22:56) Peter was walking when suddenly a servant girl looks at Peter and yells out "This man was one of Jesus followers" Peter continued to deny it saying, "Woman I don't even know this man"

Now remember, Peter is the same one who told Jesus that he would die and go to prison for him. When time came for him to stand up for Jesus he denied him. Afterward, later on down the road someone else looked at him and said" you must be one of them" Peter replied, "No, man I'm not!" About an hour later someone else insisted, "This must be one of Jesus disciples because he is a Galilean too." What are you talking about, and not only that but Peter began to curse and swear that he didn't know him. As he was saying those words, the rooster crowed at that moment and the Lord turned and looked at Peter. Peter then remembered what the Lord had said about him denying him and Peter left the courtyard weeping bitterly.

 When you are carrying the seed of God and you do not move or acknowledge the calling on your life, you are just like Peter. You may be going to church every Sunday and paying your tithes, but if the mantle is on your life to become one of God's disciples, and you have yet to move, you are denying Him whole heartily. I was the Youth Director, the Praise and Worship Leader, and even the mentor for many of the other young girls in the church. I was one of those women who stood up on a pedestal that every other young girl looked up to. If I could have put it any plainer, I was the "P. K.", the Pastor's Kid.

I allowed my salvation to be compromised for a few minutes of pleasure, some of you are denying God right now, it may not be for pleasure, but if you stop and evaluate yourself for a minute you will be able to put your finger on it. It may be due to fear, addictions, habits, situations, hang-ups, mess-ups, pregnancy, or whatever. Today is the day to admit that you messed up, and you are pregnant with a seed that only God can deliver. I missed it, I messed up, and the end result was exposure of my sin. If only I could just go back being the "P. K."

Out of the missionaries, evangelists, pastors, and prayer warriors, it's most difficult for the pastor's kids to come forth and come clean. First of all you already have people hating on you for who you are. I want to tell you that you will never be able to change who you are. Therefore, do not let others do so either. We have people who want to take away from who you are, that's why they are secretly fighting you, throwing rocks and hiding their hands. You may be at a point right now where you are struggling to stay at your parent's church, due to all natural and spiritual endurance. Stand strong until God gives you what to do and the appointed time to do it. God is not the author of confusion, but of power and of a love and a sound mind. I found myself so many times wanting to leave, trying to go somewhere else because I could not continue to take the negative battles. Nevertheless, when I stopped crying, and stopped allowing things to offend me so much or attach it to me, and grew up into a real "Woman of God" I stopped blaming my mother for not putting them in their place. I was able to stand up for myself and put them in their place. Then I was free to go forth in my ministry. Pastors' Kids, Stop and tell yourself, "I will no longer ignore my seed Lord, help me to push..."

On the way to the hospital, there was nothing but silence. My mother was focused on getting an answer as we continued to drive to Methodist Central Hospital. I was terrified of being told "you're pregnant."

While traveling in our long beige 15-passenger church bus, all I could think about was "I'm pregnant, now what?" As we arrived at the hospital, there were no parking spots and this frustrated mom dearly, I turned to her and said, "mommy we can leave since we can't find a space." We kept driving around in circles looking for a spot, just when I felt like we were going to leave, instantly a parking spot became available. I looked up to the sky and I thought to myself, it's over now. We put change in the meter and headed across the street. As we walked in, I sat down as my mother signed me in and I waited for them to call my name.

I know sometimes it's scary in the spirit realm when you find out that you are pregnant. The same system applies, you're getting nervous and your palms are sweaty. You are in shock and sometimes ask the question, why me? , or why now? God knows your destiny; He knows the seed that's on the inside of you. Ask me how I know, because He planted it! It sometimes can be a scary thing realizing that the seed of God has impregnated you, and all kinds of feelings start to run through your head; what am I going to do? Am I going to be a good carrier of the Word?

Let's just for a moment look at Mary, she was a carrier of the Word. One thing about Mary was that she was chosen to carry the seed. Just like we did not all choose to carry this gospel, but the gospel chose us. If we go to the Word of Matthew 1: 18-25 Mary was impregnated by the Holy Spirit, at this time she was engaged to be married to Joseph. But while she was still a virgin she became pregnant with the Holy Spirit. Joseph, her fiancé, being a just man decided to break the engagement quietly and quickly so she would not be disgraced publicly. In days of the Bible, a woman who was engaged to one man, and get pregnant by another man would be stoned to death (the woman and the man who impregnated her). So I believed that Joseph loved

Mary so much that he did not want her to be stoned to death so he decided not to openly announce her pregnancy. While he was thinking upon this, and considering breaking this engagement he fell asleep and an angel of the Lord appeared before him in a dream and told Joseph do not be afraid to go ahead with your marriage to Mary; for the child with her has been conceived by the Holy Spirit and she will have a son and you are to name him "Jesus". He will save his people from their sins. All of this happened to fulfill the Lord's message through the prophet, saying that a virgin will conceive a child. She will give birth to a son and he will be called "Emmanuel" (meaning, God is with us). What I like about Mary is that it did not matter how old she was, Mary had favor. There are plenty other women who want the gift that God has bestowed on you and you are impregnated with God's seed. God is depending on you to come forth. He could have chosen anyone else, but yet He chose you! Stop, just for a moment and say, "Favor Is Fair." I hear people say all the time how favor is not fair; I disagree, if you live right, you deserve the favor.

What is favor? Favor is goodwill; Let me tell you something, there were a lot of people who wanted to come forth in my place there were a lot of eggs that had passed through your mother's fallopian tube. There were some La Wanda's, Natasha's, and La Quna's and all of them were eager to come forth, yet none of them did God allow to connect with your Father's sperm. Why, because as He looked at all those eggs that had passed through your mother's fallopian tube, none of them had what God was looking for; He was looking for a woman who would love Him with all her heart, mind, body, and soul. The Lord is searching for women who He can plant a seed on the inside of, and that woman can push and make that seed come forth. He is searching for that woman who exemplifies obedience, integrity, and perseverance. Yes, there were a lot of them that wanted to conceive my seed, yet God was not satisfied with them. He chose you, He wanted you. Just touch yourself, and say He wanted me.

Just take a few seconds and encourage yourself and say He wanted me, with all my hang ups, flaws, mistakes, disappointments, He still wants me. Tell God "thank you" for conceiving inside of me. Slowly every other egg that is coming down your mother's tube, I can see God just looking and waiting on that yielded vessel to come forth. Disappointed as all the other eggs (women) race by, He still did not see whom He wanted to impregnate. All of a sudden slowly coming down my mother's tube, every egg had passed me by. That's why the bible says "The race is not given to the swift or to the strong but to the one that will endure until the end." (Ecclesiastes 9:11) Let me tell you something, I might have been the last egg slowly coming, but then God saw me. He was almost ready to choose someone else, but then came you, slowly coming and unsure if you were going to make it, But you're here looking and searching for direction, purpose, and promise. Yes, your mother's body carried you, but she had nothing to do with choosing you. God chose you. If some fathers had it their way they really wanted a "boy" but because God chose you before you were in your mother's womb. That's why you had to come forth.

In the bible, Jeremiah was a chosen vessel; God had already predestined him to come forth. (Jeremiah 4-5) Then the word of the Lord came unto me saying "before I formed thee in your mother's womb, before you were born I set you apart and appointed you as my spokesman to the world" Jeremiah did like a lot of us do; we start to make excuses about why we cannot conceive. Jeremiah tells the Lord "I can't speak for you, I'm too young" sometimes we worry about things we should not. God is not concerned with your age, He wants a willing vessel. The Lord told Jeremiah "you go where I send you, and speak what I tell you to say, and do not be afraid." Some of you there have a desire to do God's will but fear has gripped your heart and has stopped you from getting delivered.

What God is saying is that I knew you. God knows you. He knows what you will do and what you going to say.

<u>To know means to:</u>

1) Hold information in the mind

2) Have encountered somebody or something before

3) Recognize differences

4) Identify somebody or something by characteristics

<u>Jeremiah's excuses</u>

1st: He thought that he could never obey God because he was a shy and timid young man.

2nd: He told the Lord that he could not speak to people because he was a child.

3rd: Jeremiah had hinderous-false safety staying in one place-stagnated-no productivity-fear-intimidation-spiritual death

So, what I'm trying to say is that it's not by accident that God chose you. You may say, "How can I be used by God because I was an unwanted pregnancy" There is no such thing as an unwanted pregnancy, because God knew you before intercourse took place. God is in control of everything; therefore, if He did not want you to come forth all He had to do was speak against your delivery. Since He allowed you to come forth even if you were unwanted by one parent or by both parents you're still here, why, it's not because of you, but because of God.

Tell yourself there is a reason why I am here. I must deliver! You may say I was given away or my parents gave me up for adoption. You may feel like you are alone and unwanted, or maybe find yourself in a relationship that is hard to cope with or untrustworthy. Maybe right now you feel codependent on someone else. I want you to know that we share a father and one thing about my daddy is that He will never leave you nor forsake you. People leave, things leave, and relationships pass, but God will never leave you. God will always be there for you day and night, He will never leave you alone. You may say, "I was a rape victim" and feel like you have no purpose, meaning, or destiny; however, you were brought forth you cannot change the method in which you were conceived. I know you feel like you were conceived through an act of violence and right now you may want to be withdrawn or detached from society or even ashamed, But it is good to know that through all that pain God still chose you. He still allowed you to be birthed. There's a song that says, I cried my last tears yesterday. What does it mean? Yesterday was full of hurts and pain.

Yesterday I had to deal with uncertainties in life; yesterday I had to deal with who I was, who I am, and who I am going to be. A little crying is alright, but I want you to know this, people will sometimes look over you, underestimate you, try to overthrow you, try to make you feel like you are worthless, uneducated, you may at this very moment feel like the black sheep of the family. Listen to me closely my sister let them laugh. You may not have that fancy car, diamond rings, mink coat, a mansion or a house, but what you do have is something much greater. You may be saying, "what do I have that is much greater than all those material things?" That one thing you have is laughter. People who try to intimidate you right when they are trying to hurt you, make you feel bad, break-out in laughter, and tell them "The same thing that makes you laugh will make you cry." What do I mean? Go ahead girl, laugh at me, and laugh at my car, my clothes, my fears, my children, and my mate. Let them know life is funny. What goes around has to come back around, one sure fact you will reap what you sow; Good or bad, it's coming back to you. Laugh now at me, because you'll soon cry later. My translation of the 37th verse of Psalms is that you are going to get yours. It tells you not to worry about the wicked. Don't envy those who do wrong, like grass, they will soon fade away. Trust in the Lord, and do good, do what you know is right to do. Commit everything you do to the Lord. Be patient, be still, and don't worry about the evil ones. In a little while the wicked will disappear, you will look for your haters and they will be gone. So let them laugh, get the tissue ready to pass, because the same things that make us laugh, have a funny way of coming back to you and making you cry.

We are waiting at the hospital. Finally my name was called. I believe we waited about 2 hours before we were called. Some of you are in the process of waiting, and God hasn't spoken anything yet. He just has you waiting. While you are waiting, I don't want you to get tired, weary, or disappointed. Sometimes we move too fast and we cause spiritual wrecks or accidents in waiting at the red light, and you feel like you have been sitting to long, so you move along before it's your time, now you have caused an accident, you have jumped into someone else's lane. Some of you are in the process of waiting. God hasn't spoken anything to you. He has not sent a word to you. You're praying, fasting, and meditating but not one word from the Lord. If connection must take place, and if conception must take place, it is then, and only then when God speaks and says that it's time. You must wait on God's timing. Take a moment and tell yourself "not until God is ready." This is the reason why a lot of women of God do not achieve or succeed in their ministry. It is because they feel that bubbling or that pushing on the inside and before God can allow them to give birth they go on their own and have a spiritual miscarriage. One thing about God, He knows you and what others can or may not ever see. He sees. God is waiting on you to come forth. He may have to purge you, prepare you, equip you, educate you, build you, anoint you, correct and chastise you. He might even have to give you boldness, understanding, wisdom, patience and compassion. There are people who forget who they are and the things that they have done, and quickly throw judgment upon someone else. Remember Yourself! You may still be waiting, but you made it to the waiting room. Your name has already been called. Your name has been crossed off the waiting list, and if by chance you have not been called. Thank God, you are on the waiting list!

As I went in the back they placed me into a room. I was told to put a gown on. I stood there naked and ashamed. Who does that remind you of? Yes, that's right, Adam and Eve. Before they were disobedient they did not know anything about being naked, but after disobedience took place they knew that they were naked. Here comes Jesus, He is looking for them, and asked Adam where he was, Adam responded and said, "We hid from you because we were naked."

There I was naked and ashamed, asking myself why I allowed myself to be exposed. I took the entire test that they had administered to me, blood, urine, x-ray and ultrasound. I knew that soon my results would be coming.

My mother remembered at that time the parking meter would be up soon. She did not want to get the "boot" or a ticket therefore she left to check the meter. She said "I'll be right back I'm going to put some money in the meter." When she left even though it was for a little while, I felt a sense of relief. The doctor walked in, look like he was looking for my mother, then I told him I was ready to hear my results. I was lying on the bed with their cover and pillow. I sat up to hear my results and I believe at that moment my heart had skipped several beats. I even thought I was going to faint, but I didn't. He stated "you're just pregnant." Oh my God, everything in the room started to spin, my blood pressure went up. All I could think about was what I had just heard "positive". My mind started racing "how was I going to tell this Christian woman, my pastor and last but not least, my mother. I knew she would be disappointed, shocked, angry and heartbroken all at the same time. Well, being 18 years old at the time, I told the doctor that I wanted to use my right to privacy; therefore he could not tell my mother. I put that patient-confidentiality on him, which means he didn't have permission to open his mouth. With trembling in my hands and shaking feet I saw my mother. I jumped on the bed, laid down with the sheet, blanket and pillow. I pulled the gown off under the bed and put my street clothes back on under the hospital bed. My mother was looking at me strangely. I could tell she knows that something is wrong, but I kept on covering up. That is what happens to most of us as women of God, we get exposed. God tells us that we are pregnant with his seed and yet we keep hiding and covering up.

She had this puzzled look on her face as if saying "what happened?" She said very slowly "did the doctor come back in yet?" I said yes; she said "well what did he say?" I said, "We will talk about it when we get home. I know that you are tired, let's go." She started getting very uneasy and frustrated; I could tell by the tone in her voice. As I kept telling her "I'll tell you later", all while praying to God that the discharge papers would come on any minute now. The more upset she got the louder she became until finally, the discharge papers arrived and we could go home.

With the papers in my hand, I was getting ready to walk from the back to the front exit front door, here comes this nurse who knew nothing about me using my confidential-privacy act, opens up her big mouth and she says "congratulations grandma." Oh, father, my mother's head turned so slow like some horror movie, "The Exorcist," and she said "could you repeat what you just said". The nurse opened up her mouth proud and loud and said it again; "you are a grandma." She looked at me. I open my mouth then, now remind you I do not stutter. I said, "mom-mom-mommy I'm pregnant."

As we were leaving the hospital my mother stopped at the pay phone, put money inside, hands the receiver over to me. I'm standing there puzzled. I said "who am I supposed to call? With this stern look on her face "she says call the daddy." I called my daughter's father on the phone. I told him that my mother wanted to talk to him. He sounded surprised, he said "for what!" Before I could tell him my mother took the phone and told him that he needed to come to the house because we were at Methodist Central Hospital, "Georgia is pregnant!" I left the hospital that day pregnant and exposed.

Admit that you are Pregnant!

The first step to being pregnant is to admit it. In a short time you will not be able to deny it any way. There is no way to hide naturally that you are pregnant. Your symptoms are there. Just to go over a few symptoms you may become bloated, throwing up, swollen, cranky and emotional. Well let's look at being spiritually impregnated.

During Natural Pregnancy You Sometimes Experience:

1). Food Cravings- You may have a strong desire for food that you don't usually eat. This could indicate that you are pregnant.

Now let's look at cravings in the spiritual realm- you will feel that nudging of God in the direction of full-time services to God. When I say craving I mean the desire to read your word, the craving to study the word, the "crave" to become more acknowledgeable to his word.

2). Mood Swings- It is common for women to be on an emotional ride. It takes some adjustments to all the new changes that your body is experiencing. Mood Swings in the spirit are much different. On Monday you know God has called you; by Tuesday, you are a little uncertain. Wednesday, you are questioning whether you heard the Lord right; on Thursday, you deny that you are called. Friday, you feel the call again. Mood Swings come when you are battling with who you are and saying thing like, "Should I walk in obedience-at the point I am happy." "Should I wait to be sure" at that point, I am confused yes he called me. I'm excited, I'm not qualified, I'm sad so yes you will experience mood swings. However, you must learn how to cope with the new lifestyle of carrying a seed. There will be days when things are not going so well, you are a carrier of his word so you must continue to carry it on.

Spiritual pregnancy is the same way. There is no way you can ignore it: the dreams, visions, the mantle, and the tears, pushing, and tugging. When you hear the call, then you must answer. You know that there is something different about you; now when you go to the club you are not as excited to dance or move. Now when you smoke or drink it's not as much fun as it was before. The best way to stop the pulling, tugging, and having the visions and dreams that are constantly coming to you, is to simply say "Lord, I'm pregnant with your seed, help me to deliver." When you are ready to deliver then to ask the Lord "where am I called to deliver (serve)." You need to ask the Lord "is this my assignment?" "What am I supposed to do with my seed?" "Where do I serve you Lord?" These questions, for most women, are very hard to ask and very hard to answer. You must be under the leading of the "Holy Ghost." You do not want to be out of place in ministry. You must spend time with the Lord to understand your call; what I mean is that you must spend quality time with the Lord. When you stop and spend quality time with the Lord you will know what direction you are supposed to take. There are going to be times when you feel unworthy, unqualified and yet you still have to push.

Secondly, you must be patient. People often hear the voice of the Lord and before he can complete the work, or tell the whole assignment that he has for you, you run without proper instructions. You must be patient, and you have to wait until God gives you the okay. Sometimes it may take weeks, months or even years, but yet, you still have to wait.

Thirdly, seek counseling. Tell your Pastor or your leader that God has impregnated a gift on the inside of you. You have to allow them to become your covering and lead you in the right direction.

Fourth, get involved. Start operating in the calling of your gift. Start walking in leadership. Last but not least, embrace your ministry. You have to welcome every aspect of ministry, or call on your life. Run to your assignment! Do not hesitate. Don't look anywhere but up. I look to the hills for my help.

Leaders are Born to Serve

When God calls you to lead, that does not mean that you are no longer a servant. Jesus would always humble himself. When the disciples were with Jesus he showed great leadership by being or acting in servant hood. Jesus washed the disciple's feet, now remember, he was Jesus and yet he showed the leadership as a servant. Foot washing was regarded as to be so lowly of a task that it could not be required of a Hebrew slave. John the Baptist states "I am unworthy to untie even a sandal of Jesus", which indicates great humility. As a sign of exceptional love, a disciple might wash the feet of his master, but here Jesus the Master above all Masters, "The Great I am", doing the job of a servant. In John 13:1-17, Before the Passover celebration, Jesus knew that his death had come; he knew it was time to leave this earth. Jesus showed his disciples what true love was. It is a blessing when you have a leader that can and will serve you.

Here Jesus was with knowledge that Judas had already planned to betray him. He got up from the table, took his expensive robe off, wrapped a towel around his waist, poured water into a basin, and then he begin to wash the feet of his disciples and wipe them off with the towel around his waist. Jesus told them "since you call me teacher, and I have washed your feet, follow my example and wash each other's feet. How true it is that a servant is not greater than the master. When God calls you, or impregnates you to become a leader, remember every great leader once was a follower and every great follower was a humble servant. Learn how to become a leader, and yet be a servant for God.

Leaders Walking in the 5-Fold Ministry

The fivefold ministry gifts are the different examples of how God uses us and also it's an extension of ministry of Christ Himself. In Ephesians 4th Chapter, Paul was telling the people of God to have unity in the body of Christ. Paul was telling the people to be humble, patient and peaceful. He stated we are all one body, but we should all have one Spirit. Paul states that God has given us all a special gift. God is the one that gave these gifts to the church.

1st Ministry was: The Apostle

An Apostle is woman or male who builds the church. Many people love to call themselves titles that sound good. However, an Apostle is a builder, which means "One sent forth." Apostle's build new ministries, makes sure that truth is displayed, they lay the foundation in the church, they keep unity in the church, set things properly in order, oversee new ministries, and mainly they provide guidance and directions to the other Pastors that are under their umbrella. Apostles should be great leaders to follow. It should not always be about "my fellowship" and how many churches I have in my fellowship. It's not about how much dues you collect quarterly, but it must strictly be about helping other leaders to exemplify great leadership. They are to build churches with a spirit of Excellency.

<u>2nd Ministry is The Prophet</u>

Prophets always are to move by the "Holy Ghost." Prophets are to make sure that they are hearing from the Lord. In 1st Corinthians 14:3, one who prophesizes is helping others grow in the Lord, and are encouraging and comforting. Prophets are true to edify, exhort and console. Prophets, true prophet, can tell you, under the direction of the Holy Spirit, your past, your present, and your future. A person who speaks a word of prophecy strengthens the entire church. When we are pregnant with the gift of prophecy, you must only say what God gives you to say. Do not add to it, or take away from it. Remember we are not the "wonder" Jesus is the wonder!

<u>3rd Ministry, the Evangelist</u>

An evangelist is a person who brings the good news to unbelievers. Evangelists are people who actively call other people to respond to the message and to commit oneself to Christ. Evangelists sometimes call revivals, tent services, prayer meetings, or whatever it takes to

win the lost. Evangelists spread the good news of Jesus.
It is preaching the gospel, communicating God's
message of mercy to sinners

4th Ministry, a Pastor

Everyone wants to have their own church and be
recognized as a "Pastor"; however, this job is not always
peaches and ice-cream. A pastor is the watch person
over your soul. A pastor is a person that helps you to
grow spiritually, so they have your spiritual interest at
heart. They will tell you when you are wrong, no matter
how many tithes and offerings you pay. A pastor should
fulfill God's ordained purpose on their lives when it
comes time to train church members or to become
mature Pastor's. They must also exemplify the
compassion or even more than Jesus had for the people.

5th Ministry Teachers

A teacher is not a person that tries to make you shout. A
teacher is a person who brings instruction to the body of
Christ. Jesus was a teacher, He made things plain to

people with little understanding. He spoke in parables; therefore, there would be no lack in understanding. Teachers instruct men and women concerning their faith and discipleship. The church is also a teacher. It teaches us about:

1). Jesus-It presents the basis details of Jesus' life and ministry, his death, burial and resurrection.

2). Christian Spiritually - The process of growing faith through prayer, bible study, meditation and spiritual reflection.

3). Christian Ethics - This means faithfulness, morality, honesty and integrity. Ethnics, is not a law but a way of life.

4). Christian Doctrine, the truth. It opens up scriptures to determine those doctrinal ideals upon which the church is founded. It guided faithful Christians to become mature in their faith, so that they will not be "tossed to and fro."

Other Gifts One Might Possess:

1). Administrational – Is one who guides over, or proceeds over to ensure order. This person must be directed, and led by the "Holy Spirit."

2). Faith - Vision – Is the ability to believe God for everything. There is a gift of faith, were you have no doubt you simply believe and not waiver.

3). Knowledge – Understanding the truth.

4). Wisdom - The ability to make decisions. Wisdom is also the ability to make the right choices. With wisdom, you will be able to handle certain situations better.

5). Exhortation - To encourage, strengthen, exhort; to build up and to edify.

6). Discernment of the Spirits - Have you ever been around someone and you felt their spirit. You knew that it was not right. Discernment is a gift to judge or evaluate, distinguish other people's spirit. No matter what they are telling you, your discernment is never wrong. Follow the spirit.

7). Service of the Gift of Helps - Some people just have the gift of helps, Where they just love to help and meet the needs of other people.

8). Interpretation of Tongues - the ability to translate unknown languages and instruct others regarding what is being said in the tongues.

9). Miracles - the ability to perform acts that only God himself can perform.

10). Healing - the ability to change the physical, emotional, and spiritual levels of and individual.

There are various gifts, but one spirit. Each gift comes with being obedient to God. These gifts are to equip God's people to do his work and build up the church and the body of Christ. God has placed these gifts (seeds) in your life, activate, cultivate, and allow your seed to grow.

Operating in the Spiritual Gifts:

As you walk in the order of the Lord there are nine spiritual gifts. When God places a seed on the inside of you, you must know about the spiritual gifts. What are spiritual gifts; they are the skills and abilities which God gives through his spirit to all Christians, which equip Christians to serve God in the Christian community. There are different kinds of services we offer to the Lord; however it is service we offer to the Lord. It is the service to the Lord we serve. Spiritual gifts are given to us to help build the church. There are different gifts that God operates in our lives. However it's always the same giver of the gifts.

I Corinthians 12:8-11, tells us about 9 spiritual gifts:

1). Words of Wisdom - ability to give wise advice.

2). Word of Knowledge - Special gift of knowing.

3). Faith - Special faith, where an individual can believe God for everything.

4). Healing - Power to heal the sick.

5). Working of Miracles - power to perform miracles

6). Prophecy - gifts of prophecy - able to tell the past, present, and future.

7). Discerning of Spirits - ability to know whether it is really the Spirit of God or another spirit that's speaking.

8). Divers of Tongues - ability to speak in an unknown tongue.

9). Interpretation of tongue - interpreting what is being said in tongues. It is the Holy Spirit that distributes these gifts. He and He alone decides which gift each person should have.

Fruit of the Spirit

What are the fruits of the spirit? The spirit of Jesus which are in Galatians 5:22: love, joy, peace, longsuffering (patience), gentleness (kindness), goodness, faith, meekness (humble), and temperance (self-control). When you follow the directions of the Lord, you will have these fruits. If you see that you are walking in any other fruit, other than those that are listed by God then ask God to give you a good fruit. Life and death is in the power of your tongue. You can choose to except your seed, nourish it and go forth, or allow yourself to let you seed suffocate, withdraw, and die. You are pregnant, yes God told you to go forth, yes everyone else see your pregnancy. But are you going to push or allow your seed to die. Conception is here, you've already conceived, now you're pregnant, you can't change that say to yourself, "I'm pregnant now what" Push your seed and get ready to deliver.

Chapter 2

<u>Fertilization</u>

I'm Pregnant now what?

Fertilization:I'm Pregnant now what?

After becoming a new parent, with Chastity, my first born: I had to learn how to nourish, take care of, protect, and to guide, but most importantly to allow my seed to grow.

There are different types of births, or should I say labor. After five years of mothering and learning how to put someone else first, I had suddenly found myself experiencing the same symptoms from when I was pregnant with my first born. However at this point I had asked for God's Forgiveness and dealt with my sins and short comings. I rededicated my life to God, got married, and got pregnant. There I was 24 years old, hearing the doctor say once again, you're pregnant. And I said to myself, "you're pregnant, now what?" There are so many types of pregnancy. Also like in the natural, there are so many spiritual pregnancies.

 First we will talk about natural Birth, the choice is yours. Some people do not have any medicine or numbness; they would rather go through Lamaze class and learn how to breathe, to deal with the pain.

Well, at this point, I never wanted to experience natural child birth again due to the extreme pain from before. Just like you chose rather you're going to have the medicine or not, being impregnated by God is also a choice. Even though God wants you,

you must be willing to be used. It is your choice, God is not going to throw Himself, nor is glory on you; you must first be willing to let the past go. I had to deal with the fact that I conceived my daughter out of wedlock. I had to deal with carrying a seed for nine months; however I had to forgive myself, let go and enjoy my seed. When I found out that I was pregnant once again, I was overjoyed because I remember the doctor saying, "You'll be back like all the rest of the teenagers within a year." I looked at him and said, "NO, I will not, I will be married next time. "

Feeling prejudged and categorized by this doctor, I made a promise to myself that I will not be back. When you are young, you say thing that are so blurry and cloudy. I had planned a life with my oldest daughter's father and suddenly, he was gone. False hopes, had been built up, but reality had stepped in. I remember calling and calling him and his mother would always say that he was not there. I got depressed and all kinds of feelings were racing through my head. Weeks had passed by and I went to the mall with my mother, I was shopping around in Sears and there he was, shopping. I smiled and walked over to greet him, suddenly I was approached by his wife, (Yes! I said his wife!) He had slipped off and married someone else. There I was empty and alone, pregnant with his seed and he decided to head in another direction and marry another woman.

I had to realize that First you must realize that you must put away any old, self-image of yourself.

SAY WITH ME: "I am kicking the old me and embracing the new me!"

It is very important to see yourself as God sees you. We must not allow the devil to fool us into thinking that we are unworthy to carry Gods seed. If I would have allowed the devil to continue to whisper his lies, I would have been defeated.

<u>To embrace the new you, you must:</u>

1st Control your mind:

Say with me, I must control my mind.

How do I control my mind?

I must protect it, which means that I cannot allow anything to travel and reside in my thought pattern. It is Satan's job to work in your mind. When he comes to deceive you he will always start in the mind. It starts with a thought then it becomes a stronghold. Control your mind by bringing every thought in to captivity. Continue this every morning, pleading the blood of Jesus over your mind, Cast out doubts, fears, jealousy, compromising, and any spirit that controls your mind. You must know that the strategies if the enemy will kill, steal, and destroy your seed before it can manifest itself. The devil is continuously on his job, he gives demons orders to try and detour you from producing your seed. If Satan can get his demons to abort or make you lose the seed, then he feel that He can stop God's ministry. The devil is a liar, even if we never acknowledge or give birth to the seed that will NOT stop his work.

Right next to you is a woman who is praying to get impregnated or to have implantation of the seed. There is always someone else who is waiting to carry, I was in a place where I was once again pregnant; I could have easily gotten depressed. Let's look at depression for a moment.

Depression

Most women, when they are pregnant get depressed about small things, their weight, stretch marks, bloating, the emotional rollercoaster, however depression is common. Depression will take you to a dark and lonely place in your mind. Depression causes people who are in good physical condition to not be able to get up out of bed, to not be able to interact with others, at times it even causes marriages to fail. When you find yourself stepping into that dark place, do not just lay there.

Get Up Take Action!

Deal with the stress; address what is causing the emotional imbalance in your brain. Sometimes we as women do not like to be confrontational. We like to hide things and pray that they blow over, but you must stand up and confront whatever situation that has you nonfunctional. Deal with it head on. It is an individual's right to be confrontational in any situation, be confrontational, sometimes you have to be; I'm not saying be loud or a drama queen, I'm simply saying, deal with your pain.

Out in Jesus name

Speak to it: when you are ready to fight or be confrontational, you must open up your mouth and speak to that situation. You first must realize you are in a battle, we can no longer sit with our hands folded and allow the devil to steal or even kill our seed. (Ministry)

Forgiveness

You must be able to forgive. We sit year after year and we hold on to words, gestures, hurts, and pains. All while we are holding on to that abuse as a child, that unfaithful husband, that disloyal friend, and those disobedient children. We find ourselves bitter and unhealed. You must forgive, the word tells us to forgive70 x70 times daily. Satan has an advantage over you and your seed if you hold on to things and don't forgive. The less you give him to fight you with the less he will have. Do not give the devil the tool of unforgiveness to work with. I use to carry bitterness and unforgiveness in my heart. Later seeing the individuals who caused me such great pain, they were praising the Lord and happy, and unmoved by what they had done.

There I was, bitter, broken, unable to praise God and fragile, allowing hurt to eat me up like cancer, then I realized that you cannot hurt me unless I give you the power.

<u>Battles You Will Face</u>

<u>First battle :</u> Emotional battle, persistent problems due to anger resentment, hatred, jealousy, rejection, depression, fear, worry, insecurities, and inferiorities.

Let's look at rejection; maybe someone rejected you and you allowed it to settle in your spirit, therefore you think harshly or little about yourself. You are a person who has an inferiorities complex about yourself. You are embarrassed about your look, hair, shape, anything you can use to lower your self-esteem; you have to remember that the creator of all creations took time to create you. So what if you look a little different, you were made in the eyes of God. For the word of the Lord tells us that we are beautifully and wonderfully made. So, when you see someone voice their opinion on you. You tell that individual, "I am God's masterpiece and this is how God saw me, everything that God made, he had a vision, so I am God's vision."

Next we will talk about insecurities. After divorcing my first husband, I thought I found what I had been searching for. My first husband was a saved man of God, yet he had jealousy issues, due to both of us being in ministry, I knew that we would support each other; "I'll amen you while you amen me", well it did not happen that way. He found the need to sit on me while I sang, or walk out while I preached and also infidelity. My seed would've died if I had not gotten out of that marriage. I was being made to miscarriage my seed (word). I did not want to be in competition so sometimes I did not preach and made excuses to allow him to shine. With insecurities, I married a second time; I knew that he did not love God the way that I did, but we know how we do, we think that we can change an individual.

To any woman who believes that you can change anyone, you are sadly mistaken. Change comes from within. After being lied to and cheated on, I missed it, this was not of God! This man lied, got a woman pregnant TWICE and continued to live a double life. That's why the bible tells us not to be unequally yoke with nonbelievers.

I had to experience hardship and embarrassment, due to the choices I made. I'll tell anyone, to live by the choices that they make. After divorcing for a second time, I listened to the voice of the Lord, and married my soul mate, however I came with baggage. I would look in his wallet, search his phone, ask where he had been, interrogate him, and even smell his clothes all due to past hurts. I truly thank the Lord, for my man of God, Bishop Ralph Ward III, he allowed me to be insecure, and did not get mad or upset with me, he allowed me to deal with my past and stood there as my promising future.

Second Battle – Mental Problems- confusion, loss of memory, mental torment and doubt. The devil will try to make you confused about who you are and whose you are. He'll make you question your salvation. He'll try to make you doubt your seed (ministry).

Third Battle – Mouth and Tongue – gossip, nagging, lying, criticism. He'll make you use your tongue as a weapon. In James the third chapter the word of God tells us (James 3:5) *Even though the tongue is a little member and boasteth great things, behold how great a matter a little fire kindleth*; what does this mean, it means that the tongue is a small thing, but it can do enormous damage. A tiny spark can set a fire. Your tongue is like an ember of fire. It is full of wickedness that can ruin your whole life. It can turn the entire course of your life in flaming destruction. You can tame all kinds of animals, but the tongue cannot be tamed. It is uncontrollable, evil and full of deadly poison. Sometimes it speaks praises and sometimes it speaks curses. That is why we must be stable in what we say. James also tells us to not be double minded. (James 1:8) *man is unstable in all his ways, which means that they cannot make up their minds, they waver back and forth in everything they do,* a person like that should not expect to receive anything from the Lord. Use your weapons; power, authority, prayer and faith.

Motivate Yourself

Encourage yourself. There were times when I was doing the will of God and pushing to do his work.

Everything I had done seemed to go unnoticed, therefore I had to realize that I had to take my own hand, put it across my shoulders and encourage myself. First, I had to start speaking the right language, stop speaking negative things over your life.

Don't allow anyone else to speak negative things over your life.

Do something, exercise your abilities. Visualize your success see yourself doing well. Set goals, start planning your future. Think Big you may be living in the basement now but have Penthouse/mansion thinking. Don't allow people to stereotype you, due to how you look, dress, or your personality. My hair may be straight, it may be wavy, braided nappy, or weaved up, however God sees me for who I am. Big hips, little hips, big butt, round face, it does not matter, He sees only me. People who judge others simply for their outward appearances, judge wrongly and you must destroy any spirit that tries to attach itself to you to make you feel less than Gods best.

Let's Pray

Father, I come to you in the name of Jesus, I come to you for my sister (say the name), I bind the spirit of (call that spirit out), that has tried to attach itself to her, I speak life in Jesus name, Get up my sister, the seed is there, Push it out.

Bounce Back

We sometimes wonder if we can come back from all the hell we've been through, where it seemed that we are in a dead situation. Looking at my clothes feeling like I have my grave clothes on and my situation is stinky, but I am reminded of Ezekiel 37th chapter. "My God, I feel the spirit of the Lord, woman you are about to live." There Ezekiel was and the Lord had taken him by the spirit to a valley filled with bones. Ezekiel saw old lifeless bones all over the ground. They laid there, scattered everywhere, lifeless, no hope, and no joy. GOD spoke to Ezekiel and asked him, "Son of a man, can these bones become living people again? "Ezekiel said unto the Lord, "you alone know the answer to that." What I love about this is that Jesus told Ezekiel, he had to do something; you can't just sit there and drown in the flood of problems, you must speak to them. He spoke to the bones, he said, "dry bones, listen to the word of the Lord, I am going to breathe into you and make you live again." All you have to do right now I lift your hands right where you are and tell the Lord, Breathe on Me!

The Lord said I will put flesh and muscles on you and cover you with skin. I'm going to breathe into you, and you will come forth. So Ezekiel began to prophesy to the bones, all of a sudden, there was a rattling noise all across the valley, the bones of each body came together and attached themselves as they had been before. While Ezekiel was standing there, muscles and flesh formed over their bodies, and skin formed to cover the bodies, but still, no breath had been breathed into them.

See, you may be recovered you may be past the hurts and pains, but breath has not yet been spoken. Then he spoke;

"Breathe into these dead bodies so they may live again." As he spoke the wind entered the bodies, so they began to breathe.

They came to life and stood up on their feet, and they were alive again.

You have to take authority and speak life, people have written you off. They see your situation and have already pronounced you dead, they have written you obituary, they have sang the last hymn. I want to tell you woman of God, tell them stop the funeral! I will live and not die. Look at Jesus; it does not matter to him, whether or not the situation is dead or not.

Looking in Luke 7:11, Here was a widow woman, she only had one son. In the time of the bible, a widow was treated like an orphan. They were mentioned to be fatherless. Orphans were often referred with widows as representatives of the most helpless members of society. Without a father or a husband you were considered a social misfit, without anyone to provide for their material needs and represent their interest in court life was harsh. They were forced to beg for food, they suffered the loss of their homes, land rights, livestock, and were sometimes subject to violence and treated as property to be gambled for; However God has a special concern for widows. God has warned the people not to take advantage of them.

Luke 7:12 here, this funeral procession was coming, this young boy had died, the only son to this widow woman. Many mourners were there with her.

Isn't it funny how when you are down or in a dead situation, there are many people around you. Why? People like to see you where you're down. It's a sight to see. They are ready for your destruction, they are planning for your fall, and they are ready for you to die! They are ready to see you in a spiritual casket. They're ready for you to be pronounced dead, but I want you to let them know that you are going to live.

As Jesus saw her, he had compassion, He said, "Don't Cry", he walks over to the coffin and touched it and when Jesus comes on the scene, everything that is dead has to stop and immediately come to attention. Pallbearers had to stop, the mourners had to stop, and the spectators had to stop, when God speaks to your dead situation, everything that's dead has to stop. Jesus said to the young man, "Get Up!" and the boy got up and began to talk to those around him, and Jesus gave him back to his mother. I want you to pull those grave clothes off and live!!

Here I was going through pregnancy again! However I knew what to expect because I had been through this before.

Acknowledge Your Seed

There are women right now trying to help out in other areas. You're that Usher, you have a special way of greeting people and you make sure the offering line is right. You make sure the children are not being distracting and see that is order in the church. You have your pretty black and white on, or your all white, your pretty white shoes, white gloves, and stockings to match. You can direct traffic with the guidance of your hand, believe me you are the best usher you could ever be, but lately you feel like ushering isn't enough, Lately you hear the voice of the Lord more clearly. You feel the urgency to draw just a little bit nearer. You've been feeling the presence of the Lord just a little bit harder. You feel the spirit just a bit more often than usual. When you pass the programs out, now you feel the anointing in your hands, what does all that mean to you? It means that you're pregnant with Gods seed. You were not just called to be an usher you can continue to serve, continue to pass out the programs and direct traffic, but I speak to you womb, that usher, yes you're that usher that's hiding in the back of the church, but God sees you, yes he wants to use you. When everyone else walks past you and sees so little, God sees a whole lot more. That's why the bible tells us to be careful and not to offend the least one. Admit today, that there is more in your spirit, preach the word, woman of God.

Now run to your pastor and tell them, I'm pregnant with a seed (ministry), pastor, please help me deliver."

You must be that awesome choir director; nobody else can direct a choir like you, no one else can swing their arms from right to left. No one can inspire men and women to open up their vocal chords like you. You can transform scared, timid, shy women and men to confident singers. The pastor loves to see you direct, he compliments you every Sunday. The choir praises your gift and talent. You know how to bring that exact song to practice that will set the church on fire from Sunday to Sunday. However, deep inside there is more you sit and hear the word preached, Sunday after Sunday every word is deposited in your spirit. When you feel the call of God, tears roll down, when the preacher asks "will you be a willing vessel?" you sit there, completely still because of fear, doubt and unbelief. Yes, God can use a choir director to preach his word, sometimes God will allow you to start off as a choir director, but your praise has taken you to another level. You will always remain in the basement when you are afraid to advance or go on to the next level. So I say to that choir director. Keep singing, keep inspiring, yet you must direct yourself to the call. When you will not do that, God has a funny way of showing you that someone else will.

I remember God allowed me to experience that one Sunday. I was asked to sing and I said no. later in that service, someone else got up and sung that very song that I was asked to sing. Believe me, when I tell you the church went up, it was on fire, people were crying and the spirit came in at that moment. God said, "If you will not do it, I have someone else who will", therefore if you want to keep hiding behind that pretty choir robe, do so, but you know and I know, that ministry is now. Look at your hands, say with me; "What's in my hand?" you're just like Moses, all of the time the gift was in Moses's hand.

Look at Exodus, God wanted to use Moses for a very important task, to be the voice that spoke to Pharaoh, telling him to let the people of Israel go.

Exodus 4: 1-17, if I may paraphrase this, Moses was a man who God had chosen to go to Pharaoh. God told Moses that he had heard the cries of his people. He's seen taskmaster being harsh and he told Moses, "I want you to go the Pharaoh and tell him that I said let my people go." Moses started telling God, "they will not believe me; they will not do what I tell them to do."

Verse 2 is what I wanted to focus on; and the Lord said unto him. "What is that in thine hand?"

I really want to ask you, my choir director, what's in your hand. God showed Moses the many miracles he could do with his hand. You may have healing in your hands it's not just for directing. God has placed so much more in your hand. Moses, like you started to make excuses like, "well God I'm not a good speaker, please God, I've never been a good speaker, I'm clumsy with words, I stutter." God asked Moses, "who makes the mouth; who makes the people so they can speak or not speak." Moses again tells the Lord to send someone else. You cannot keep making excuses unto the

Lord. Choir director, what's in your hand? It's a gift, it's an anointing, Push your seed.

Next, we have the First Lady, you're so beautiful, with your nice suit, your diamonds on, your shoes, your hat, your mink coat. Everybody recognizes you as the first lady. You love to stand and be acknowledged as such. You've gotten comfortable just where you are, but God needs more. He wants the seed (ministry) that's on the inside. There Hanna was she wanted to become pregnant with a seed, and sometimes you sit and see other women going forth and you want that, I mean you're not envious or jealous; you've just gotten to a point where you want more. Here Hannah believed that she had gotten to a place where she wanted more, she was barren for many years. She vowed to the Lord that if she could give birth to a son, she would dedicate the child back to God. If I was to say anything to you First Lady it would be the phrase of a Blues song my eldest daughter was singing one time and it caught me with these words; "People see me but they just don't know." Yes people see you, they see the fine clothes, diamond rings and the outward smile, but if they just look a little harder, they will see the real you , they will see the hurts, the pains, and the frustration. Everything that they think is glamorous really is not. Everything that shines is not gold. It is very different being married to a Pastor or Bishop; I know being married to one myself. She was praying to the Lord. Eli, the priest, saw her lips moving but couldn't hear anything so he though she was drunk. He approached her and said, "You come to the Lord's house drunk, Throw away your wine!"

She tells the priest the priest, "I'm not drunk, I'm just sad, I was pouring my heart out into the Lord." Sometimes you have to pour your heart out unto the Lord, you can't worry about make-up running, clothes getting wrinkled, or what others think or say, you must cry out unto the Lord.

God is Evicting Me!

One night, I was at home and I heard the Lord say to me, "I'm getting ready to evict you", at the time I did not understand, because I lived in our family house and no rent was collected at the time, yet the Lord kept saying, "I'm going to Evict you", now, I know what evict means, it means to put out, not by choice but by force. Since it could not have meant natural, it must have meant spiritually. After I really got an understanding of what He was saying to me, I understood, He meant I am forcing you to move. When you are pregnant with Gods seed (ministry) God does not have time to wait until you decide to be obedient, therefore He will allow you to go through things that will cause you to forcefully move, let's look at Jonah, a man of God. Jonah was evicted to carry out seed (ministry). God told Jonah to go to Nineveh, and announce his judgment on them, due to the wickedness of the people; Jonah decides that he is going to go the opposite direction in order to run from God. How many know that there is no hiding place.

He went down and to the sea coast, to the port of Joppa, (Jonah1: 1-17) where he found a ship that was going to Tarnish. He bought his ticket and hopped aboard. When God wants to evict you, he will find you wherever you try to run. God found Jonah on the sea, He allowed a violent storm to come, and they began to throw items overboard to lighten up the ship. They started praying to their Gods. In all of the commotion Jonah had the nerve to be asleep down in the hole. The captain came and asked him, "how can you sleep, we're about to die. The captain told Jonah to get up and pray to his God. When they got the bottom of whose fault it was and why they were in the situation they were in Jonah confessed and told him that he was running away from God. The sailors began to get terrified because the storm was getting worse. They looked at Jonah and asked him, "What should we do" Jonah tells them, "throw me overboard, and the sea will calm down." The sailors tried to row harder, but the storm kept getting more and more violent. They picked Jonah up and threw him into the ragging sea. Immediately the storm ceased. God was getting ready to Evict Jonah; He allowed a great fish to swallow Jonah, Jonah stayed in the mouth of the fish for three days and three nights. After God evicted Jonah (forced him to move), the bible says that God ordered the great fish to spit up Jonah onto the beach. What was supposed to be a three day journey, turned out to be a one day journey, Next time God evicts you, you'll learn to move faster.

Say with me:

Lord, I will obey you; you will not have to evict me to move. I will move voluntarily, on my own.

Don't make God Evict you! No Eviction.

Who's Pregnant?!

There are people waiting around right now and they claimed that they didn't know they were pregnant. I watch this show, and it's called" I didn't know I was pregnant" Now I don't know how your period has stopped, your feet are swollen, you've gained or lost weight, your appetite has changed and you're irritable. You've had all of these symptoms, and you say you don't know that change is happening to you.

Who are you? Come to yourself!

There are times when we forget who we are, that causes us to settle for less. Take for instance "the Prodigal son", he decides that he's grown and no longer wants to follow his father's rules.

Let's look at Luke 15: 11-32. This man has two sons, his younger son tells his father, and "I want a share of your estate now." He decides that he does not want to wait until his father's death. So his father divides up the wealth between his eldest son, and his youngest all out of timing. We can know that we are pregnant with Gods seed, yet we want the fame and the glory so fast. We want spotlight and pulled back curtains, applause and all of the screams of recognition all before time. So he picks up his stuff and travels to a distant land, and there he spent all of his money on wild living. Just having himself a ball, but soon the money ran out.

Say with me, Just an amount of time, all that you are doing that contradicts the word of God will come to an end. It's fun doing what you will and what you want, but at some point all that grace and mercy will run out. A famine came through the land and he began to starve. He convinced a farmer to hire him to feed his pigs. He became so hungry that the pods he was feeding the pigs looked good to him, but no one would give him anything, but at home he had everything. While he was down there feeding the pigs, hungry, thirsty, weak, he comes to himself, you need to come to yourself. Get up from that low place, get up from that slime. Do you know who you are? Do you really know who you are? I believe he asked himself if he knew who he was

He began to say to himself; at home even the servant has some food to give me, if I stay here I will die of hunger. He said "I'm going to go home to my father, and tell him that I have sinned against him, and against God. I'll tell him, I know that I am no longer worthy to be called your son, please just let me be a servant." It means something to God if you tell him that you messed up and you know that you are no worth to be called his.

While he was returning home ready to humble himself to a servant, his father saw him in the distance coming home, yes you've made up in your mind you're coming home and God sees you coming, he's getting ready to meet you, the angels are rejoicing for him thinking that you have to lower himself, he confesses to his father, but his daddy ran to his son and embraced him, and kissed him. He told his servants to get him the finest robe, get him a ring for his finger, get sandals for his feet and kill the fattest calf so they could have a feast. When you know who you are, you may go through, however that will not change you.

Favor is Fair, God favors me!

Different people in the bible experienced Gods favor. If I could talk about Esther, Daniel, Enoch, David and Joseph there are many more, but I'll just name a few.

What's a favor? Favor means exceptional kindness, special reward, and goodwill. Sometimes God has to remind you that he favors you. That you are his favorite, I was in my second marriage, finding out later that I had been cheated on more than 100 times, and not just with one woman, with several women. I had gotten a hold to my ex-husbands phone and there were over 20 different women in his second hidden phone that he had been intimate with. When I finally caught him over the other woman's house, I immediately thought about "what about AIDS or HIV." I was so scared I took my mother to the health department I was thinking that my life was over. All I could think about was who would be a mother to my three children. I went there, took a number, scared, mad, and betrayed all in one. They called my name, I went to the back, they took blood and urine, and at this point I wanted to be tested for everything. I was sitting there thinking, "What will the diagnosis be" By this being my first time, I didn't know that they gave you a number and you had to call back and get your results. While I had time to wait, I just meditated on the Lord. My mom went with me and we were in the waiting room, I'm telling my mother I knew something was wrong. She tried to encourage me and she said, baby, people live with HIV and Aids," they have medicine so you will be able to live a normal life. I'm with you, your sister and brother are with you, and we all support you." At this time I'm still thinking that I'm not strong enough to deal with something like that, but when I called, I gave my number and she said, "You're negative". I asked her if she was sure and she said yes. She said not just negative for one thing, but I was clear of all diseases. So when I think about how God spared my life out of all those women he slept with, without condoms, God protected me. That's Favor. Say with me: Favor is fair! Later learning that the woman who had the affair with my ex- husband died, right after giving birth to their daughter.

Esther was a Jewish orphan girl who was chosen over all virgins by the king to become Queen, when his wife Queen Vashti, refused to come and show off her beauty at a banquet hosted by her husband, he wanted all of the men to gaze at her beauty, for she was a very beautiful woman. After Vashti embarrassed her king, he was furious, therefore he ordered that she be banished, and that he should choose another queen more worthy that her. Esther was chosen due to favor. Esther Lived a hard life, being an orphan living with her uncle Mordecai, but God so granted her favor.

Let's look at Daniel, he was chosen by king Darius to become one of the administrators that supervise the princess and watch out for the king's interest. The God allowed favor to rest upon Daniel. He soon proved himself more capable than all of the other administrators and princes because of Gods Favor, the king made plans to place him over the entire empire. Then the other prince and administrators began searching for some kind of fault that they could put on Daniel. Maybe the way he was handling the affairs, but other than that nothing. He was faithful, honest, and responsible. They thought to themselves, "The only way we can get to Daniel was through his religion." They plotted and schemed against Daniel, they knew that he prayed three times a day, so they went to the king and got him to sign a decree that could not be broken. For 30 days, no one could pray to any God or man except for the king, or they will be thrown in to the lion's den. The lions were untamed and always ready to attack. The king, not knowing their deception, signed the decree. Daniel continued to pray to God as always, he went home, knelt down in his upstairs room with his window open toward Jerusalem. He prayed three times a day just as he always done, giving thanks to God. The haters (officials) went to Daniel's house, observed him praying, asking for Gods help. They went back to the king and reminded him of his decree. They told the king that it was Daniel, the king got upset with himself because he knew he had been tricked into signing the law. He spent the rest of the day trying to save Daniel. The officials kept pushing, but how many of you know that favor is fair. You don't need money or anything else materialistic all you need is favor, favor works when bad credit fails, it works when the doctor has given up on you, all you need is favor. At last the king gave the orders to have Daniel place in the lion's den. The kind said "Daniel may your God, whom you worship save you." A stone was brought and placed in the mouth of the den. No one could rescue Daniel from the lions. The king went back into the palace, upset, fasting, he refused entertainment, and he couldn't sleep at all. He got up early that morning and ran to the lion's den. He called out for Daniel, "was you God able to save you from the lions?" Daniel answer, "God sent his Angels to shut the lion's mouth, so they could not hurt me."

Daniel was freed from the lion's den, it was nothing Daniel did, and he just kept serving the true and living God. All you have to do is keep serving God. Do not compromise your salvation for no one. In a time of trouble God will show you favor. Enemies were all around you but favor had your back. You know that you've gotten some stuff that you didn't deserve, you have gotten some positions that you were not qualified for, but favor allowed you to get that job without a proper education or a degree.

Vengeance is the Lords

You don't have to worry about your enemies; the Lord will take care of them. Here was Daniel, a smart ambitious man, with great wisdom. He had the gift of faith, he was a great dream interpreter, the outer appearance was handsome and well groomed, he wrote in two different languages and last but not least he showed great courage. You should not waste Gods time worrying about enemies.

Enemies, you are always going to have them, there will always be someone that finds something that they do not like about you. You can find two haters and they will never dislike the same thing about you, but vengeance is the Lords. Just like that old song that says "Jesus will work it out when I give it over to the Lord" in other words, when I remove myself from the situation and I turn it over to the Lord, he will work it out.

While they were plotting to have Daniel killed, they could not have known what was in store for them. Daniel was not worried about serving man. He served the true and living God. Daniel learned of the decree and was informed about the law being signed. The Administrators knew that Daniel was a spiritual man and all the dirt they tried to get on Daniel, they could not find any to put on him. All that they had was his religion and his relationship with God. They plotted together to fool and trick the king to sign his decree, all of the time they had their own selfish motives. Without knowledge of their intentions the king signed the decree.

Daniel was, a man who loved the Lord. He went home and knelt down as usual in upstairs room, opened up his window toward Jerusalem, and prayed to the Lord three times a day, just as he always had done. The Haters went to Daniel's house and found him praying.

How many of you know that the enemy will set you up, they get what they thought was dirt on Daniel and they went back and reminded the kind of the Law he had signed. The kind tried everything he could to fix what he had done, with no other choice king gave the orders for Daniel to be arrested and thrown into the lion's den. Not only that but a rock was brought and placed over the den. The king had faith, he looked and Daniel and said," May the God whom you worship get you out of this." The king was so upset that he couldn't eat, he couldn't sleep, and he refused to have his usual entertainment.

Say Out Loud: But vengeance is the Lords and I shall repay.

Here Daniel was, in a situation that looked like death. It looked like it was all over for Daniel. He was thrown in a den of lions and not just any lions, wild lions that were always ready to kill. But when favor rests upon you favor will step in just in time. Early that morning the king got up, expecting a miracle, activating his faith, yet he did not know it. He called out to Daniel and Daniel answered, Daniel told the king that God sent angels and shut the mouths of the Lions so that they could not harm him. Vengeance is the Lords.

Not a scratch was on Daniel.

<u>**Vengeance**</u>

Gods vengeance did come forth; when you try to bring harm on someone else God will step in for you. The king gave orders to arrest the men who plotted against Daniel. He had them, their families, their wives and children and threw them into the loins den. Before they could even get to the bottom of the pit the lions leaped up and tore them apart. You don't have to worry about what your enemy is doing, just trust God.

Enoch is another example of Gods favor. Enoch lived with such a close relationship with God that he was transported into the presence of God without dying. Enoch just disappeared because God took him up. How awesome is that, no funeral, no burial, no body, God just allowed him to vanish.

Last example of favor is Joseph. Name meaning "adding"

Joseph was the eleventh of twelve sons. As a child of Jacobs's old age and Rachel's son, Joseph became the favorite and was given a coat of many colors. A long sleeved , richly ornamented robe given to him by his father. (Gen: 37.3) This and dreams which showed rule over his family inspired by the envy of his brothers who sold Joseph to a caravan of Israelites, Joseph was later taken to Egypt, where he became a trusted slave in the house of Potiphar, an official of the pharaoh. While there Potiphar's wife decided that she wanted to sleep with Joseph. Joseph refused her, so she made false accusations against him, therefore he was put in prison, but Joseph received favor. He went from the pit to the palace. Favor is fair.

Sometimes God has to remind you of his favor, you know you used to be a drunk, tripping and falling all over everyone, your friends who used to drink with you and maybe got more drunk than you, have liver problems, they have aged and even have heart problems, but the favor of God has spared you. There is nothing wrong with your liver, or heart. You did not have to go to any A.A program, God just sobered you up. Tell yourself "it's nothing but favor." You know you used to hang with the wrong crowd, doing all kinds of illegal things, but while everyone else was getting caught and going to jail, ending up having warrants, yet somehow your name was never mentioned. God hid you, it wasn't because you were so slick or smart, it was because of Gods favor.

Why? It's because the world is taking their own lives and having nervous breakdowns. Why have you not lost your mind, why have you not tried to kill yourself? It's because of Gods favor. You're going through hell and misery, yet you have not yet thrown in the towel, it's due to Gods favor. How is it that innocent people are getting hit by stray bullets and dying every day, but you have had guns in your face and the trigger pulled, but the gun got stuck and

God spared your life? It was nothing but favor. Tell me why when you were doing drugs, shooting up and sharing needles and smoking more than your heart can take. How come you're smoking buddy or someone who smoked more than you, died of an overdose or got brain damage, yet you are still here to live and tell that drugs kill. What is that? "I'll tell you it ain't nothing but favor".

Just stop and tell God, thank you for favor!!

How is it that you and a close friend have the same sickness and their sickness, tears up their lungs, heart, and liver, and destroys their cells, breaks down the muscles and contaminates their blood, yet your illness had no effects on you? That is called favor.

How is it that a person that tries cigarettes for the first time and smokes for only two months, ends up with lung cancer and throat cancer, but you have been a smoker of over ten years, God deliver you from nicotine addiction and your test come back and show no cancer. "Baby, that ain't nothing but favor."

If I could stop and give my testimony , how is that a women's husbands cheat on them one time, and they bring their wives back, AIDs, HIV or any other STD. yet I find out, in my ex marriage, I was cheated on over 100 times with several women and prostitutes. Two children were brought in on me through this marriage, yet every time I went to the doctor, no diseases. That was nothing but favor, when you live right favor is supposed to come forth.

These are some benefits of favor:

1. Prayers are heard

2. Receiving life

3. Mercy from God

4. Health

5. An escape plan

Therefore God had chosen you. You're no longer surprised, the initial shock of hearing you're pregnant has worn off. Now, what are you going to do about it?

I'll tell you what you're going to do about it. You're Going to get your vitamins, your iron, your physical and your due date. After which you must begin to love your seed. You start by trying to eat a balanced meal. So change your eating habits and start exercising to keep your body in shape, everything and anything that will allow your body to love your seed.

Let's look into the spiritual side; so many people eat from so many different tables. Every time there is a prophet in town, we run to that service, we find ourselves always eating spiritually from so many tables that we are harming our seed. When you are naturally pregnant, when you mix too many facts together, what happens? You get sick, you're vomiting, your stomach is running off and you have a fever, because you have mixed too many ingredients together and you found out all of the flaws would not mix, but you have to love yourself enough to protect your seed. Tina Turner's song said it best; "What's love got to do with it?"

What is love?

Love is unselfish loyal, concern for another. Just like when we cater to and include our natural fathers to our natural seed, we must continue to include our spiritual father to our spiritual seed. In the New Testament "King James version uses the word charity, charity comes from the Latin word "caritas" which means darkness, affection or harsh regard. Love can be described as self-giving among family and friends just as we are overjoyed with the natural father in our lives that helped produced our natural seed. We tell everybody that we are extremely happy. We pray that the son has his father's eyes, nose, looks, and actions. As women, we are proud of that, but when our spiritual father hands a seed to us, we find ourselves close-mouthed, doubtful in our heart, and unsure in our spirits. Yes, there are people who will hate on you for being impregnated by God and you ask yourself why. It is so obvious why. Jesus said that he commanded us to love one another, most importantly; you have to love your enemies, and pray for those who persecute you. What do you mean first lady? It means you have to love those who say you are not qualified or say you don't deserve it or God has not spoken to her. Those folks you have loved. Loving those who love, that's easy, but when you can love those people who laughed at you, lied on you, plotted against you, mislead you, hurt you, misrepresented you, then and only then will you be ready for your assignment. People sometimes use the slogan "I'll forgive you, but I'll never forget". When you continue to hold grudges and ill will feelings for people who have wronged you, then you will never grow.

What's Love got to do with it….Everything?

Let's talk about a mother's love. Solomon was a wise man, and wisdom fell upon him greatly there were two women in the bible, both had a baby, both carried this seed inside of them for the entire time. Both women went to sleep with their babies. When morning came, one mother woke up to discover that her baby was dead, she was deceitful, and she switched her baby with the other mother. Early that morning the other mother got up and noticed that the baby was dead, but as she got a closer look at her seed she realized that that was not the seed that she produced. She realized that the children had been switched. The case was

brought to Solomon and he used his wisdom. King Solomon said,"
I'll tell you what I will do, I'll cut the baby in half, he looked at one
mother and said, you have one half and she'll have the other half."
It's something about a mother's love, the real mother of the child,
spoke up quickly and said, "No, don't do that I would rather the
child to live, give the baby to her". However the other mother said,
"yeah that's good", eager for the destruction of someone else's
seed, but a mother's love stepped in, she would rather give up
their seed to see it live. Solomon's wisdom kicked in and he said
"this right here is the real parent," and the child was placed with
its rightful mother. Sometimes people will try to steal your seed,
they can imitate you, they can fool other about you, but when
wisdom comes, the truth will be revealed.

Who's Carrying the Seed?

There are so many women that that God wants to use, yet you
don't know who you are carrying. Just like the King Solomon used
wisdom. You must ask God to give you wisdom.

Wisdom is a revelation given to a believer by God, the ability to
discern the purpose and plan of God. True wisdom will tell you
how all about order, so many times we get up in church services
and we really don't know what to say, and what not to say.
Wisdom teaches us, if we are asked to sing, not to preach,
wisdom will tell you how to conduct yourself. Wisdom will tell you

if you're supposed to tell someone something or simply pray about it. Wisdom teaches you when to talk and when to listen; wisdom teaches you to guard you tongue. Wisdom teaches you how to handle someone how to guard you attitude wisdom help you develop your character.

Therefore, I was pregnant again, but this time married in the right relationship with God, yes I experienced the prenatal , yes my body went through the changes and I said to myself, "Girl you're pregnant, now what." There was nothing more I could do but enjoy me seed. On July 25th 1998 I had my son, Elijah Deonte Walls, a healthy baby boy. And this labor was easy, but every seed is not the same. I look at my seed every day and I thank God for my seed.

Pregnant now what?

The first thing you must do is watch the enemy; he's always trying to snatch someone seed.

You must first be:

Alert, so many people are sleeping in evil times. First Peter tells us to be sober, be vigilant because your adversary, the devil, walks about like a roaring lion, seeking whom he can devour.

What does this mean? It means that the devil is always trying to find someone who he can turn away from God, and when you're so focused on the natural, you miss the spiritual walk. You must stay focused; you must continue to walk with assurance that God placed that seed on the inside of your womb. You cannot be un-alert. You must be awake and focused.

Chapter 3

Denying the Birth:

What to do when you believe you are carrying a seed?

Denying the Birth: What to do when you believe you are carrying a seed?

I was watching this show on television one night. It was titled "I didn't know I was pregnant". Women would go through all the symptoms of being impregnated, yet, they still ignored the signs. They did not get to enjoy the stages of childbirth, because they were not sensitive to the changes that their bodies were going through.

After having my son, Elijah, I thought that my child bearing experience was over, but to my surprise, I found myself pregnant again. However, this time I did not recognize the symptoms. I didn't feel the normal morning sickness, fatigue, or weight gain, none of those things did I feel. However sitting in my den one day, I started to have great pain, and great discomfort.

I asked my mother to take me to the hospital because I had severe stomach cramps, bleeding, and sweating. I could not for the life of me figure out what was happening. My mom stated, "Do you think that you are having a miscarriage?" I answered undeniably, "There's no way I could be pregnant." Denying the birth was so easy due to the fact that I wasn't ready for another child, and I thought I had taken the necessary prevent me from having another child. We made it to the emergency room. They rushed me to the back, and the nurse said, "You are having a miscarriage". "Miscarriage," I yelled, "I didn't even know I was pregnant." I haven't even gone for my six weeks check-up yet, how could this be? I am serious I was in a true state of shock. My body was doing its own thing, and I could not control it. I looked up "miscarriage birth"; I found out that a miscarriage is the spontaneous abortion of an unborn child prior to the 20th week of a pregnancy. Causes for a miscarriage are numerous. Frequently, miscarriages occur before the 12th week of pregnancy about 20-30% of pregnancies end in miscarriage. These tend to occur in the first two to three weeks of pregnancy, and usually are due to the lack of the embryo to implant. In the natural "miscarriage pregnancy", whether the woman knew she was pregnant or not; if a miscarriage happens, it occurs whether you are knowledgeable of conception or not. Therefore, when your body goes through a lack of a developmental process of fertilized eggs in the uterus that may sometimes causes abnormalities that cause miscarriages.

<u>Spiritual Miscarriage</u>

A spiritual miscarriage is a lack of something, like faith. Everyone needs faith. The word of the Lord tells us, that it is impossible to please God without faith.

What is Faith?

Hebrews, the eleventh chapter tells us all about faith. It allows us to know that faith is the substance of things hoped for, the evidence of things not seen. What does all that mean? Faith, is when you believe what you cannot see; it's the assurance that what we hope for is going to happen. The entire universe was formed as God commanded, that's what we know. We know that it didn't come from anything that we have seen.

"Examples of Faith"

It was by faith that Enoch dying; suddenly he disappeared because God took him. (Hebrews 11:5-6). It was faith that Noah built the Ark on. He built the ark to save his family from the flood. He obeyed God, who warned him about something that had never happened before, the Flood. (Hebrews 11:7)

Spiritual Miscarriage (Lack of Faith)

Luke (1:23) at this time Zachariah who was a Jewish priest. Zachariah had a wife, and her name was Elizabeth. Now Elizabeth and Zachariah were righteous in God's eyes, so very careful to obey all of the Lord's Commandments. However, they had no children due to the fact that Elizabeth was barren, and they were very old. She was past the age of child bearing. While Zachariah was in the sanctuary praying, an angel appeared to him, and told him that God had heard his prayers and that his wife would bare him a son. Disbelief and doubt (causes of a spiritual miscarriage) began to happen. Zachariah stated, "How can something like this happen, I'm old, my wife is too. She is way past her child bearing years." What he meant was her clock had stopped ticking years ago, and she stopped having any type of menstrual cycle. How can anything like this happen? So the angel told Zachariah, "Since you do not believe that what I am saying is from the Lord, you will be unable to speak until the child is born." But just like the Lord said, Elizabeth became pregnant and bore a son, "John the Baptist". The reason why Zachariah had to go through a spiritual miscarriage is due to his doubt and disbelief. Another type of birth is still birth.

Still Birth

A still birth occurs when a fetus, which has died in the uterus during labor or delivery, exit's a woman's body. There are so many women who face this type of birth. Even though their child is dead, they still have to go through the whole process of delivery to allow the fetus to exit their bodies. This is a "dead seed."

"A Dead Seed"

When I searched the Bible, I was looking for a woman who could be classified as a "Dead Seed." That woman is Job's wife. Let's look at her for a minute. As long as God was blessing Job, with everything he needed, wanted, or desired his wife was fine. She loved the riches, the fame, and the prosperity. But as soon as trials and the testing time came, she quickly turned on God and told her husband to do the same. Out of all the material possessions God gave her and Job, she turned on God as fast as she could. We, as women, have been taught wrongly. We have been taught not to allow the man to be the man, and what happens is we find ourselves getting out of place. We find ourselves being that unsubmissive, rebellious, nagging, and unsupportive wife; just like Job's wife was. Never did she attempt to pray with her husband. Just like we women sometimes do, we argue, we fuss, and complain. Meanwhile we don't know that we are operating with such negativity, and that we are speaking "still birth" (death), to our marriages. When we say, "I do", that brings about a sudden instant change. You are unable to hang out with friends all the time, like you used to. You're not able to just sit up on the phone, texting, or watching soap's all day. To be honest, you lose some of your freedom when you say "I do".

But Job's wife was so selfish and self-absorbed that she could not come to her husband's aid, due to her "me, myself, and I" mentality. If we do not become that "virtuous woman" we will soon see a still birth (dead) marriage.

What is a virtuous woman? In Proverbs (31:10-30), the Bible tells us about the type of woman we should long to be. It tells us that when a man finds a virtuous woman he has found something more precious than rubies. She's loyal and honest; her husband has every reason to trust her. This means she's not a liar and cheater. She's not trying to hinder him, but she is his support system. She helps him all of her life. A virtuous woman is not lazy eating chocolate bon-bons all day with rollers in her head, with a nasty home waiting for him to come to and find himself food. He doesn't have to worry about one blue sock and one red sock. She is a hard worker, energetic and strong. She makes wise decisions; she's a person who knows how to budget. She watches for bargains, she knows how to make her husband shine. She knows how to speak well. Her husband praises her, the children call her blessed. She realizes that beauty and charm will fade, but she's a woman who fears the Lord, and prays daily for his guidance. She realizes that her will is God's will for her life.

What is will?

There are 3 different types of wills:

1. The Direct Will: The order of the Lord; it is not the permissive will; it is the original mind in the heart of God which commands (guides) us, to follow.

2. Permissive Will: Is self-will; it's when he permits us to do, after our persistent and continuous asking.

3. Satan's Will: to kill, steal, and destroy.

When you do not obey the direct will of God you will find yourself in "Spiritual Abortion". Natural Abortion is termination of pregnancy. It is the removal or expulsion of a fetus or embryo from the uterus resulting in or causing death. Let's look at Bathsheba.

Spiritual Abortion

Spiritual abortion can also be called a "Bad Conscience". The definition of conscience is a sense of right and wrong. It governs the thoughts and actions urging an individual to do right instead of wrong. Bathsheba, a beautiful woman, was the daughter of Eliam and the wife of Urian the Hittite (2 Samuel 11:3-27). Now Urian was a Hittite mercenary; or a native, perhaps noble Israelite of Hittite ancestry in David's army. He was a member of David's Elite Warriors. Uriah's name means "fire of Yah". As the Bible tells us in 2 Samuel that David got up one afternoon late after taking a nap. So, David strolled on the roof of his palace. He looked over the city, and notices Bathsheba bathing. He was so mesmerized by her beauty that he sent for her. After they had intercourse, she discovered that she was pregnant, not by her husband, but by David. Isn't it funny how the devil tricks your mind to think there are no consequences to our actions or choices you make? So she's pregnant. They realize that they have a situation to fix. David tries to get Uriah to go home and have sex with Bathsheba, but Uriah's loyalty lead him back to the palace with the other servants. David tried everything. He got Uriah drunk, he lied, and he manipulated to get him home to sleep with his wife. When Uriah did not, David had him put on the front line, and he was killed. Bathsheba aborted her marriage. Sometimes we feel like the grass is greener on the other side, but when you get there, however, the grass is brown, dead, and useless. Bathsheba mourned for her husband, but found a way out afterwards, when she moved in the palace with David giving birth to his son. Don't abort your marriage or your relationship with God. Stay focused. Spiritual abortion is a bad decision and a bad conscience.

Don't Look Back

So many times when God delivers us we always find ourselves looking back. We pray for God to deliver us out of bad marriages, abusive relationships, financial struggles, mental issues, afflictions, and much more. God stops and we turn right back around and place the shackles back on. We must learn, when God says step out, step out! When God closes a door, we must learn to keep it closed. The word of God says, "It would have been better that you not put your hand to the Gospel plow and looked back. The word is saying it's just like a dog going back to its vomit. It also indicated, "That you are not fit for the kingdom of heaven." All God told Lot was to not let anybody look back. Sodom and Gomorrah had turned to an evil place. The cities were wicked, lustful, and unnatural. Therefore, the Lord was tired of all the evilness; so, he decided to destroy those cities. As the Lord was destroying the city (Genesis 19:23-29), Lot's wife decided to look back as she was following behind them and she turned to a pillar of salt.

Dealing with the Spirit of "Manipulation": Jezebel Spirit

Webster's Dictionary states that manipulation means the following:

➤ Exerting shrewd or devious influence for one's own advantage

➤ Handling the action of touching with the hands

➤ Control; to hold something over one's head; fudge; tamper with the purpose of deception

➢ One who obtains personal gain at the expense of other people by using them

There are several manipulators in the Bible. We sometimes find ourselves persuading people to do what we want them to do by any means necessary. Let's expose this spirit of manipulation.

Jezebel's Spirit

The opinions of a Jezebel spirit range from a sexually loose woman or man, to someone who teaches false doctrine. Jezebel is classified under the spirit of manipulation, due to the fact of the need to have "control". Her trait or character is to dominate, and control others, especially in the spirit realm. Anytime you must be in full control of others' lives, decisions, and their every move and if they feel the need to please you, and they are fearful to make their own choices, thinking that they will disappoint you; then you are operating in the spirit of "manipulation". No one person should have that much control over another person's life.

<u>**Jezebel (Manipulation Spirit) Symptoms**</u>

1.) Will not submit; must rule or be in control

   Example: an unsubmissive wife

2.) Having no control over ones mouth

   Example: backbiting, gossip, and slander

3.) Jezebel women are never happy.

- Always finding a reason to complain

- Never satisfied

4.) Women that have a Jezebel spirit make men spiritually weak.

Example: Challenging male authority; argumentative in public; lack of respect;   disrespectful openly; competitive in home or church

5.) Jezebel women cannot admit when they are wrong.

   Example: Justify their wrongs; will not except their wrong doing; will not take correction

6.) Jezebel women have false humility, and use deception and deceit.

Example: Cunning, flattery; put on a fake character to get what they want;

Unsubmissive wife, but pretend as though they are submissive.

7.) Jezebel women have selfish ambitions; they're self-absorbed (me, myself, and I)

Example: Do not care about anyone else's feelings but your own.

8.) Jezebel is very religious, but only to the cause she believes in

Example: She takes scriptures and tries to fix them according to her gain.

Many women are so eager to get married. The perfect picture wedding, yet, they are possessed by the spirit of "Jezebel". From a small young girl, I was taught how to be a wife. I was taught to be a strong woman. You have to accept the fact that marriage will change you, and as a woman you will lose most of your control. After going through 2 marriages, and now on my third, I understand that I must take some responsibility for those failed marriages. It's so easy to put all the blame on the other person. As I now think back, after being taught by new "husband", Bishop Ralph Ward III, I understand that I was an unsubmissive wife. We feel like we are going to keep that "Single=Freedom". Not so? You lose all those kicking it days. As I look back, I find myself having a lot of blame for my failed marriages. I loved hanging with my sister and my mom, always jumping in the car to go somewhere. I was leaving my ex-husband to really wander. Now I'm not saying that because I was gone, that gave them the right to cheat, yet loneliness opened the door. Plenty of times I stayed at work from sun up to sun down, like the Jezebel spirit, making sure my career was set, yet I was neglecting my children and my mate. By the time I made it home I had no energy, I was tired and broken down. I had absolutely nothing left for my family.

Control

I always felt the need to have everything my way, not really focusing on what my children or my mate wanted to do. I always had to control the atmosphere. I always had to have things my way. My house had to be designed my way. My children's lives had to be directed my way. I had to control my children's circle. They had to know who I felt comfortable with, and that's who they chose. I had to have a say so on their style of clothing. Full control was me. A part of me really felt like they were happy. But I realize now that they had been directed and guided by manipulation. You cannot choose who they will fall in love with. You cannot run their house and their home; you can't manipulate their lives, all their lives. Jezebel is a spirit, which is not of God. It is of the devil, and if you find yourself in the spirit, it's time for Deliverance.

How to Get Rid of Jezebel

1. Stop fooling yourself! If you are operating in the spirit, do not be ashamed. Admit that you have this spirit. Admittance brings forth deliverance.

2. Repent: It simply means to turn from what you are doing wrong. Start now doing what you know is right.

3. Walk in your freedom and your deliverance. You must continue to read your word; get in a Holy Ghost filled church with true believers; stay focused on God, and resist the devil.

Let Us Pray

God I come to you, admitting to you that I possessed the spirit of Jezebel. Lord, today I freely denounce this spirit from my life; I repent of my sins, and every other trait that this spirit carries. Wash me, cleanse me, and make me whole again. I accept you Lord as my Lord and savior. In Jesus' Name, I pray. Amen.

If you prayed this prayer, Hallelujah, you are now free.

The next spirit we are going to expose is the spirit of Covetous.

Delilah's Spirit

The first time in the Bible I recognized the spirit of covetousness is when I read about Cain and Abel. Let's head to the book of Genesis.

First, Webster's Dictionary tells us that the word covetousness means:

A. Extreme desire to acquire or possess

B. Resentful or painful desire for another's advantage

C. Excessive desire for more than one needs or deserves.

D. Greed for material wealth.

There are a lot of people, even in your VIP Section, or your circle of family and friends. Sadly, sometimes it can be a mate. The spirit of covetousness is always searching for an opened door.

<u>**Exposing the Spirit of Covetousness**</u>

(Genesis 4:1.) Cain was the first born son of Adam and Eve. Cain was a farmer, and his brother Abel was shepherds. The time for each man to bring their offering to the Lord, Abel's was accepted; but Cain's was not. Subsequently, Cain murdered Abel, his brother. Sometimes we, as women of God, tend to murder each other. No we may never take a knife or a gun and cause natural death, yet we kill with something much greater, the tongue. An example of spiritual murder is lying. Lying is defined as being dishonest and untruthful.

Example: Ananias and Sapphira (Acts 5:1-6)

Ananias and his wife Sapphira sold some property, and this property belonged to them. They could have chosen to do whatever they wanted to do with their funds that they received from selling this property. However, they allowed the devil (Satan) to fill their hearts to plot and lie. They brought part of the money to the Apostles, but claimed that this was the "Full Price". His wife agreed to this deception. Peter being a Man of God, full of discernment, asked Ananias, "why has Satan filled your heart?" You lied to keep the Holy Spirit, and you kept some of the money for yourself. Peter began to tell them the property was yours to sell or not. You could have done whatever you wanted to do with your property. After you sold it, you could have kept the money to yourself; Peter began to ask them, why they felt the need to lie. You were not lying to me, he said, you were lying to God. The Bible says in Acts 5:5, as soon as Ananias heard these words, he fell to the floor and died. His body was wrapped in a sheet and he was taken out and buried.

Don't Be an Accomplice

The Bible speaks about 3 hours later, here comes his accomplice, his wife. When someone is a liar, you will always find them having an accomplice. An accomplice is a person who will back up someone's lies, or stories. Once again, Peter asked, "Was this the price for your land?" Sapphira opened up her mouth and replied, "That was the price". And Peter said, "How could the two of you even think about doing a thing like this, conspiring together to let the spirit of the Lord?" He told her, "just outside are the men who buried your husband, and they will carry you out, too." Instantly, she fell to the floor, dead. She was carried out and buried beside her husband.

Consequences for Your Actions

Cain presented a gift that was not pleasing to the Lord, yet he got angry because the Lord would not accept it. Cain and Abel were brothers. Adam and his wife slept together and she became pregnant with Cain first. Cain's name means "acquisition", while his Brother Abel's name means "breath, vapor, and meadow." Abel is characterized as an outstanding person, because he was the first person to worship God, correctly. He demonstrated faith accurately, and he pleased God fully. Abel was the first shepherd to influence the early Hebrews to place a priority on the pastoral life. (Genesis 4:1-16) It was harvest time. Abel and Cain presented gifts to the Lord. Cain brought a gift from his farm produce, while Abel brought several lambs from his flock. The Lord accepted Abel's offering, but did not accept Cain's. Cain got very upset and angry. When you get angry, you sometimes experience: jealousy, envy, and strife. Cain decided that he would kill his brother. Later on he had a plan. He manipulated his brother to go with him to the field. Eventually he attacked Abel, and killed him.

Life is a Circle

I know you've heard people say, "you're going to reap what you sow. Well that could be good or bad. When you do evil to someone or ill-will someone, at some point, these things will come back on you. You sow well, you will reap well; you sow badly, you will reap badly.

Consequences for your Actions

1.   When you till the ground, no crops will come forth. That means no food will be produced.

2.   You will be a homeless fugitive on earth.

You Must Have a Conscious

One thing about Cain was he never had a conscious. After he killed his brother, he was still jealous and envious. He showed no remorse. The Lord asked Cain, where is your brother Abel. He stated to the Lord, "I do not know, am I my brother's keeper". He never once showed any guilt or sadness for what he had done. The word of the Lord tells you that the Lord chases those he loves. When we do wrong, we should have a conscious. You should feel bad about things you do that causes hurt and pain to another.

<u>**Who Causes Many People to Deny their Seed "Satan?" Who is Satan?**</u>

Many people think that Satan is this little guy with horns and a tail sitting on their left ear urging them to sin. Satan was created as an Angel. His name was Lucifer. He was described as a cherub, the highest created angel; having anything he wanted. He was able to wear fine clothes and jewels on his robe; but that wasn't enough for him. He became greedy and had a desire for more. He became arrogant in his beauty and though that he deserved to sit on the throne above God. Satan stated the I "will's". Satan knows your future and he will try to rob you and rape you of your destiny.

<u>**What is Rape?**</u>

Rape is about power, not sex. Rape is an action where a person is victimized, and forced into an action they do not want to do. Whether its sexual intercourse, oral sex, or penetration with an object.

Several Types of Rape

1) Stranger Rape: Where a person who does not know their rapist.

2) Acquaintance Rape: Where the victim knows their attacker.

3) Date Rape: Where the victim is dating the person who rapes her.

4) Multiple Rape (Gang Rape): Where the victim is raped by more than one person.

5) Marital Rape: Where the victim is raped by her husband.

6) Spiritual Rape: It is when the Devil comes in and forcefully snatches all the ingredients you have of spirituality from your body, mind, and soul. Satan comes for 3 reasons: kill, steal, and destroy. Many people allow him to "rape" them of their destiny (future), and don't try to put up a fight to save their seed.

Many victims, after they have been naturally raped, have all kinds of thoughts going through their heads. Feelings of hurt and betrayal are some of the thoughts.

Below is a list of the feelings a rape victim may experience:

Natural Rape: Victim may experience bitterness. Bitterness is one of the most common feelings that kind of selfish, inconsiderate feeling toward others. A bitter woman rejects biblical teaching. Bitter women are motivated by complaining and gossip. They have no self-esteem. Bitterness is self-induced misery. You may be a woman who has had several blows and knock downs in your life, but you must allow all bitterness to become denounced from your life. Yes, you were done wrong. You may feel like you deserved something that you did not receive. But if you want healing in your life, and want to experience the true overflow of God, you must allow yourself to let go of bitterness.

Examples of things that may make a woman bitter:

A. A barren woman: May become upset because they cannot conceive a child.

B. Suffering lack: When women don't understand why they are facing hardship and trials in their life.

Recovering from Bitterness

You must first admit that you are a "bitter woman". You must confess that bitterness has a hold on your mind. If you do not ask God to take it out, you will walk around depressed, burdened, drained (not only physically drained, but spiritually.)

Let Us Pray

Lord I come to you acknowledging that I am working in the spirit of bitterness. I no longer want possession of this spirit. I repent for allowing the devil to use me. I turn away from bitterness now, and I receive forgiveness and peace. Amen.

If you truly prayed this prayer, then, healing has just begun.

A Woman of Resentment

What is resentment? It is a feeling of displeasure, conviction, anger, or excitement by a sense of personal injury, hate, discontent, grudge, malice, envy, irritation, jealousy, or unfulfillment.

Example of resentment in the Bible:

A great example of resentment in the Bible is Leviand and Simeon, the brothers of Dinah. Now, Dinah was the daughter of Jacob and Leah. Dinah's name meant "justice" or "artistically formed". According to Genesis 34, Dinah was going to visit some young women who lived in her area. While she was on her way, the local prince, Shechem son of Hamor the Hittite, saw her. He took her and raped her. After raping Dinah, Shechum tried to win her affection by expressing his undying love for her. He went to his father and demanded him to get this girl for him because he wanted to marry her. After Jacob found out that his daughter had been raped, he waited before he told his sons. Then all of a sudden, here comes Shechem, the rapist, with no remorse for what he had done. He addressed Dinah's father and brothers. He begged for them to let him have her. He said he'd give them whatever they wanted, whatever the cost. Due to the spirit of resentment, Dinah's brothers deceived Shechum and Hamor. They told Shechem a lie. They said that if he circumcised himself, but not only himself, but every man in the kingdom, then they would agree to allow him to marry Dinah. But, how many know that when you are dealing with the spirit of resentment, it will allow you to become deceitful, dishonest, and manipulative. It can alter (change), one's personality. So, Shechem quickly and gladly agreed. They got all of the men in the town and circumcised them. About three days later, "resentment" popped in Dinah's brothers minds.

I can imagine the hurt and pain. Maybe they felt this way because she was their sister, and they weren't there to protect her. I believe that they were disgraced. They had all of these emotions going through their minds. A few days later, all of the men in the town were sore, and their wounds were still fresh, hardly bearing any energy. So, Simeon and Levi took their swords, confident of defeat without opposition, entered the town and slaughtered every man there, including Shechem and Hamor. They rescued their sister from Shechem's house and returned home. But, before leaving, they took herds of donkeys, and any and everything they could get their hands on including all the women and children.

Wow! See what the spirit of resentment will do. It will cause the most humble woman to plot and plan until she turns evil and vindictive. If you know that you have or are carrying that spirit, let's get healed, delivered, and set free. So, many times we hear the statement, "Two wrongs don't make a right", that statement is very true. What did Levi and Simeon gain by killing the whole town of men and taking their possessions? Did it change the fact that their sister was raped? No, when they finished and killing, the fact still remains that even now, decades and centuries later, their sister was still raped.

Let Us Pray

Lord, I come before you acknowledging that I possess the spirit of resentment. I no longer want to carry this spirit. I let go of all pass hurts, wounds, and anger from my spirit. Heal me; heal my mind, my spirit, and my soul. Resentment I no longer want you to be a part of my life. Loose me and let me go. In Jesus' name, Be Set Free! If you honestly meant that prayer, you are now healed from resentment. Walk in your freedom.

Dealing With the Spirit of Selfishness

What is selfishness? Selfishness and rebellion we can deal with today. Webster's dictionary explains Selfishness and Rebellion.

Selfishness: when a person becomes overly concerned with one's own welfare or interests and have little or no concern for others; self-centered

Rebellion: opposition to authority.

In the Bible another rape took place. This time it was two women who raped their own father. When you deal with the spirit of selfishness, you are dealing with an individual who cares totally about themselves. This type of person will go a far distance to get what they want, no matter who they step on.

Sodom and Gomorrah (Genesis 19)

One evening two angels came to Sodom and saw Lot sitting. He greeted them and took them to his house to wash up and to eat. Lot insisted that they spend the night, and then get up early in the morning to be on their way. Lot had a great feast for the men of God, the angels. As soon as they were all getting ready to retire for the night, all of the men of Sodom, young and old, came to Lot's house. They all surrounded his house shouting and demanding that they allow the two men to come out so that they could have sex with them.

Lot's Flee (Genesis 19:11)

The angels blinded the men's eyes so they could not find the doorway. The angels told Lot to get his family out of this place (Sodom). When Lot hesitated, (Genesis 19:16), the angel seized his hand and the hands of his wife and two daughters and rushed them safely out of the city.

<u>Lot's Daughters (Genesis 19:30)</u>

Lot later, afraid of the people, he took himself and his two daughters to live in a cave in the mountains. One day the eldest daughter, thinking only about herself, says to the younger sister, "Girl have you looked around, there are no men for us to marry, and you know daddy is getting old. Soon he will not be able to have children."

<u>Selfishness</u>

Watch this; she comes up with a plan to get her own father drunk and to have sex with him, so that she and her younger sister may get pregnant and keep the bloodlines flowing. How selfish and unbalanced can a person be to intentionally sleep with their father and purposely get pregnant by him? They were only thinking of themselves. Sometimes, we as women can be selfish. You must realize that the world does not revolve around you, but there are other people that have to be considered. We sometimes wonder why people pull away from us and our friends are involving us less and less. It could be due to the spirit of selfishness. All you think about is yourself, your feelings, your emotions, and no one else. That is a spirit that will turn anyone off from wanting to be in your presence.

<u>Let Us Pray</u>

Lord, I repent for walking in the spirit of selfishness. I realize that spirit is not allowed in my life. I ask that you deliver me and set me free from that spirit in Jesus' name. Now, Thank God for Freedom!

The Bible speaks of another rape, the rape of the "Concubine" Levite women at the hands of the men of Gibeah (Judges 19:25). In those days there was no king to answer to. A Levite man brought home a woman to be his concubine from Bethlehem in Judah, but she was an unfaithful woman and she returned back home to her father (Judges 19:2). About four months later, this Levite started missing his concubine, so he took a servant and a donkey to persuade her to come back home. After the father convinced them to stay an additional five days, the man was determined to leave with his new concubine (Judges 19:3-8). They got up, and it was late in the day when they had reached Jebus. So, the servant was a little fearful. He told is master, "it's getting late to travel, let's just stay in this Jebusile city tonight." But, the master was stubborn.

He decides that they can't stay in this foreign city where there are no Israelites, he tells them, "we will go to Gibeah." As the sun sets they are in Gibeah, a town in the land of Benjamin. So, they stopped there to spend the night. In this particular town, no one was friendly; they rested in the town square because no one would take them in. While they were resting an old man coming home from his work in the fields invites them over. While they were at the old man's house enjoying themselves, some wicked men in town surrounded the house and beat on the door shouting and screaming for him to bring the Levite man out so they could have sex with him. The old man tells them, "no don't do an evil act, therefore he offers his virgin daughter to the concubine, but they would not listen they wanted the Levite man (Judges 19:25-30). The Levite man, afraid for him, pushed the concubine out the door. The same one that he said he needed and loved, he threw out to the wolves.

Anger and Dirtiness

There are some people that have lived an angry life, who are mad at the world for their downfalls and mess-ups in life. Then, there are people who are just plain "dirty". They look forward to hurting people and destroying their character and their name. They sit, plot, and plan how to destroy individuals. They care nothing about the after effect or consequences for their actions. They are just low down and dirty.

The Men of Gibeah

As they were trying to beat the door down, the Levite threw the Concubine out to them to save himself. These men were evil; they raped and abused her all night long. They were taking turns raping her until the sun rose. Finally, at dawn they let her go. She returned back to the house where they were staying. She was so weak from all of the abuse her body had been through, she collapsed at the door. When her husband opened the door the next morning to leave, he found her face-down with her hands on the threshold (Judges 19:27-30). He picked her lifeless body up. He put her on the donkey, trying to make it home, but her husband had already known she was dead. Anger and Dirtiness will cause women to kill their mates. It will cause women to "snap". In the Bible, for forcible rape, the offender was made to marry his victim and was not permitted to divorce her (Deuteronomy 22:28-29). Anger must be dealt with; therefore you will not give praise to the Devil at all.

Deception, Force, & Hate

The last rape I am going to discuss is Tamar and Amnon. Here is a man that rapes his half-sister (2 Samuel 13:1-22). Tamar was David's son Absalom sister, and she was beautiful. Amnon, her half-brother fell madly in love with her. He was so obsessed with her that he grew ill just by not having her. Remind you that Tamar was a virgin and he knew he could never release his sexual pressure or fulfillment for her. He devised a plan (2 Samuel 13:5), with his crafty, deceitful friend, Jonadab. The plan was to pretend that he was sick, and he wanted his sister Tamar to take care of him. Tamar came to take care of him, not knowing what was on his mind. She came into the room and she started fixing the dough for the bread. Just like he planned, he threw everyone out. As she's feeding him, he grabs her and tells her come have sex with him. Tamar began to plead, and tells him no. Amnon wouldn't take no for an answer. She yells, "you can marry me, so I will not be shamed", but Amnon would not listen. He overpowers and rapes her.

<u>Anger</u>

After he rapes her, he begins to hate her greater than he had ever loved her (2 Samuel 13:14-19). He screams and yells to his servants to throw her out. Look at this. Amnon is forceful, deceitful, and now angry.

When you allow the Devil to play with your emotions, sometimes he will take you to a point of no return. There are plenty of women behind bars simply because of anger, force, and hate. These are natural examples of rape. Also, the Devil will spiritually forcibly rape you of your destiny, your prayer life, your walk with the Lord, and you're anointing. He will force himself on you. If you don't be careful, you will wake up raped and not even see it coming.

Denying the Birth

Don't deny what God as placed on the inside of you. Don't stand idle, while Satan rapes and aborts your mission. Every time we stand in disobedience, we are denying God. After I had my son Elijah, shortly after my miscarriage, I felt the same symptoms again. Yes, you guessed it, I was pregnant again. I was still in my first marriage. I had my son in 1998, I had a miscarriage shortly after, and afterwards I was pregnant again. Oh how I denied being pregnant again. On December 27, 1999 I gave birth to a healthy baby girl. I named her Ashley Tierra Walls.

CHAPTER 4

THE REJECTED SEED:

Surrogate Syndrome

THE REJECTED SEED: Surrogate Syndrome

So, I had my daughter, Ashley, and I couldn't believe I was pregnant again, but I was overjoyed and ready for the challenge. You must remember every seed that the Lord gives you, some of them, will never be the same. I have 3 wonderful seeds that I produced with God's help, and none of my children are the same. Each seed is different. Chastity is my oldest, Elijah is my middle, and Ashley is my youngest. They all have their own personality and destiny.

Let's look up the word "Barren". When a woman is barren it simply means that she is unable, for some reason, to produce. There were several women in the bible that experienced "barrenness". You may be trying all you can for God's Seed to be produced, however, you are barren. Webster's dictionary describes a woman barren as:

- Sterile: Cannot produce an offspring

- Not producing

- Unproductive

- Empty

What causes a woman to be naturally barren? If you are a woman and you have been trying to have children, there are many reasons why women can't get pregnant. A reason could be a blocked fallopian tube. Fallopian tubes are the two thin tubes on each side of the uterus. It helps lead the mature egg from the ovaries to the uterus. If your tubes are blocked, the egg cannot reach the uterus, and the sperm cannot reach the egg which prevents fertilization and pregnancy. That's the natural blockage. Some symptoms of blocked tubes are: irregular menstrual cycle, abdominal pain, unusual vaginal discharge, etc.

<u>Let's talk about Spiritual Blockage</u>

Spiritual Blockages, or "Spiritual Road Blocks", are things that will keep your tube line to God hindered and blocked. Some Spiritual Road Blocks are:

1. No forgiveness: You must forgive

2. Strongholds: You must break free

3. Sin: Sin leads to death

4. Holding on to Soul Ties: Cut people that mean you no good loose.

5. No Faith: To please God, you must have faith.

These things and more will hinder your walk and productivity with God.

<u>Spiritual Barrenness</u>

Spiritual Barrenness leads you to not producing. It does not mean that God has not released everything for you to come forth, but there is something that is causing you to be unproductive. There is a reason, spiritually, that you are in the same place. There is a reason why you can't get to the next level; you must find your blockage. Just like when your sink is clogged up, you use "Drain-O". You must find what's causing you to be plugged in wrong and drain it out. Say to yourself, "Unstop the Plug".

<u>Let's briefly talk about the women in the Bible that were barren.</u>

<u>Rebekah (Genesis 25:21)</u>

Her name means "cow". She is the daughter of Bethuel, and Abraham's nephew. Isaac pleaded and begged the Lord to give his wife a child because she was barren, and God did, He answered Isaacs's prayer, Rebekah became pregnant, she later repaid God for his miracle

Rachel (Genesis 29:31)

Rachel was a childless and barren, she was the sister of Leah. Leah could have children, Rachel, the Lord did not allow. Rachel brings us to a different topic. I'll come right back to Rachel.

Elizabeth (Luke 1:5)

Elizabeth was the wife to Zachariah. She also was barren. Elizabeth and her husband both were very old. Elizabeth's time of having children seemed like it was over. One day her husband was at the Temple praying, and an angel of the Lord appeared to him, saying "God has heard your prayers about a child, and you will bear a son." Zachariah states to the angel, "How can my wife and I have a child as old as we are?" The angel told him, "Since you don't believe the word of God, you will be speechless until the birth of your son." It pays never to question God.

Don't Question God

Due to Zachariah's doubt and unbelief, he had to face judgment. When God tells you that you are pregnant with his seed, it does not matter how many times you have failed, or if you feels like you're not ready. You have to accept God's seed, and he will allow you to deliver.

What is a Surrogate Mother?

A surrogate mother is a woman who chooses to carry a child and give birth to that child for a woman or couple who are unable to produce a child of their own. Most of the time, genetic father is the male of the married couple.

Surrogacy

Wikipedia, states the surrogacy is an arrangement in which a woman carries and delivers a child for another couple or person. This woman may be called traditional surrogacy, because she may be the child's genetic mother, or she may carry the pregnancy to deliver after having the embryo. When a woman chooses a person to become a surrogate mother, this means that they have come to an understanding that they, on their own, cannot carry a seed.

Surrogate Christian

A surrogate Christian is a person who handicaps another. Sometimes we feel as if we are helping people by praying them through every situation, yet while you are praying them through, they're at home sleeping, slobbering, and snoring. You are handicapping them to a point where they can't pray, they don't have to give up anything because you have took their seed, and you're giving birth to someone else's seed. You must understand that women of God must do whatever it takes to give birth on their own. To allow your seed to come forth, you've got to give God whatever it takes. If it takes me running up and down the aisle, I'll do it. If it takes tears flowing down my face, let them roll. If it takes me laying prostate on the floor, I'll do it. I'll do whatever is necessary; I don't need anyone to carry my seed or my destiny. I don't need anyone to give birth for me. I'll speak to my own womb, and give birth myself. Thank you for praying for me, thank you for carrying me, but I don't need a surrogate mother. I'll speak to my own womb and tell my see to come forth!

Rachel

Rachel used a surrogate mother. She was not willing to wait on the Lord, but she used someone else to give her seed life. Rachel decided that God was moving to slow for her. Sometimes we step before God. We feel like He's moving to slow, and we want to step ourselves along the way, before God and have a surrogate mother to carry for us. Rachel began to get angry and jealous hearted (Genesis 30:1). Rachel saw that she wasn't having any children; therefore she became jealous of her sister Leah. "Give me children or I'll die," Rachel impatiently told Jacob, "Sleep with my servant Bilhan and she will give me children, in order words she'll produce me a seed." So, Rachel used her servant Bilhan to be her surrogate mother. Rachel could have continued to pray, fast, and believe God, but yet she took the easy way out and let her servant have sex with her husband. This seed could never be hers.

Sarai

Another woman in the Bible that used a surrogate mother was Sarai. She used Hagar, her servant to produce her seed. All Rachel had to do was praise God and pray. Everything is in God's timing. Just like "conception", it will not take place until it's time (Genesis 30:22). God remembered Rachel's prayers and gave her a seed that she gave birth to and named Joseph. Sarai decided that she could no longer be patient, and she could no longer wait on conception through her own body. She had to use someone else's body to carry a seed for her. Therefore Sarai used Hagar (Genesis 16:1). Sarai was Abraham's wife and she could not bear him any children. She begins to tell her husband to use her handmaid Hagar. She told him to have sex with Hagar so that she might produce them a seed. Abraham takes Hagar and sleeps with her. She conceives and gives birth.

The Downfall of Using a Surrogate Mother

In the natural, surrogate mothers are costly and they can drain a family dry. They can play on their emotions, due to wanting a child so bad. In Sarai's case, Hagar began to act funny and mistreat Sarai. She started to throw it in Sarai's face that she was pregnant and Sarai was not. Sometimes when you try to use surrogate people, they will come back after they've produced the seed. That's why it's important to let women conceive, produce, and give birth to their own seed. While you are waiting for God to allow you to conceive, you must praise your way through.

What Does Praise Do?

Praise confuses the enemy. It allows you to communicate with God. We are commanded to praise God. It is not by choice, but you are ordered to praise God.

Different Types of Physical Praise

a.   Clapping Hands: Clapping your hands is an expression of happiness and joy. It also is a way to smack the devil in his face.

b.   Standing: This is a sign of respect. Some people just want to reverence the Lord. To show him their respect, sometimes people stand.

c.   Marching: When Jericho marched, the walls began tumbling down. Marching is an expression of victory.

d.   Dancing: You don't have to wait for God to pick your legs up, and make you dance. When you begin to leap, you will feel the shackles and chains falling off. David danced out of his clothes. Sometimes we have to shake ourselves loose.

e.   Lifting of Hands: When you lift your hands, it's a sign of surrendering yourself to the Lord. You are telling God, I let go and I give up. I freely follow behind you, and I freely hunger for you. When you lift your hands, you are telling God, "God, here I am, do what you must."

f.   Bowing or Kneeling: Because we reverence the Lord, we sometimes bow and kneel before God. When the fire of the Holy Ghost falls upon you, there are times when all you can do is bow or kneel.

g.   Silence: This form of praise, we must realize, everybody does not praise God the same, and there are some people who become silent before God. Hearing his voice and following his own direction.

h.   Tears: Tears are a response to experiencing the love of God comes, there are people who tears just began to flow, nobody's hurting and bothering them, but the inward love for God begins to flow outwardly through our tear duct glands and they flow.

Giants Will Fall

Giants are examples of "A Seed That's Rejected".

What Are Giants?

Giants are any of a race of huge beings of human form who fight with Gods. Giants are imaginary beings of human form, but of the superhuman size and strength; a person or thing of great size and intellect.

<u>**Different Giants**</u>

1. Fear: It holds you back from fulfilling your purpose.

2. Intimidation: When you feel that everyone is better than you.

3. Poverty & Lack

4. Sickness

5. Disobedience

6. Stress & Worry

7. Controlled by the enemy

8. Sin & Addictions

9. Old Habits/Your Past

10. No Self-Control

11. Low Self-Esteem

12. Jealousy/Betrayal

13. Old Hurts & Wounds

Anything that causes you stagnation is considered to be a giant; anything that will not allow you to move forward is a "giant". Giants will cause you to have a disadvantage. Giants are weights and handicaps that cause you to be unfruitful and unproductive in a dry place; they cause you to not be able to move ahead.

The Challenge

You must understand that the Devil will try to challenge your faith in God, which means he will try to deny the true power that you know God has placed on the inside. Goliath was David's giant. He was bigger, and tougher. David was simply bringing his brothers roasted grain, and ten loaves of bread. He told him give ten cuts of cheese to their captains. David's brothers were in Saul's army

(2 Samuel 17:1). Here Goliath was making the challenge. Goliath was a Philistine champion. He was a giant measuring over nine feet tall. Goliath was so confident that he could beat every person up. He stood and shouted across to the Israelites, "We don't need a whole army to settle this battle (2 Samuel 17:8), he said, "Choose someone from your side to represent you and I'll represent the "Philistines". "If your man can kill me, we will be your slaves," he stated, "but if I kill him, you all will become our slaves." Saul heard this and his army was terrified. Every man was terrified of the giant. They all feared how big and scary he looked. Every day he came out to challenge the Israelites. David walked by and heard the challenge. He asks, "What is the king willing to give for the giant's death?"

<u>**Accept the Challenge**</u>

You must be confrontational; you must not allow the Devil to continue to bully and harass you. When he tries to remind you of what your weakness is, remind him what his weakness was and how it became his downfall and his defeat. David is looking at the giant, yet he knows the God he serves. So, David, a little shepherd boy, accepts the challenge (1 Samuel 17:32). David tells Saul, "I'll fight this giant." You have to come to grips with yourself, that you can no longer get bullied, punked, and thrown into a corner; you must fight.

I remember when I was younger and every day I had a bully who wanted to fight me. I would say something back, but always run into the house. One day, I was over "Madea's" house. She was a blind lady who had great ears; my bully stayed two houses down from Madea's house. The bully came to Madea's house and I was ringing the doorbell screaming to get in. Well, that last time, I believed that Madea got tired of me running. I pulled and pulled on Madea's door with no response. I know she heard me, yet she didn't respond. My bully stood eye-to-eye with me, toe-to-toe. The challenge is accepted, and the fight is on.

The Fight Is On

(1 Samuel 17:41) David starts outward to meet Goliath. David picks up five smooth stones. The only thing that David was armed with was his shepherd's staff and sling; he started across to fight Goliath. Just like me, I walked toward my bully, ready to fight. When I showed signs of strength, fearlessness, and focus, my bully left and stated, "I don't want to fight you now, I'll fight you later." As Goliath moved close in to attack, David ran quickly towards him. He reached in his sling, and hit the Philistine on his forehead; the stone sank in.

Just Satisfied

Saul was satisfied in allowing David to put his life on the line. He did not ponder over whether or not David would win (1 Samuel 19:9). Eventually, Saul allows his jealousy to persuade him to kill his "surrogate mother". David is playing the harp, and Saul hurls his spear, trying to kill David, but David dodges and moves out of the way.

Moses Used Aaron as a Surrogate Mother"

He tells the Lord all kinds of excuses about how and why he's not qualified to do the will or the work of the Lord. He tells God in Exodus, "I'm tongue tied, and I stutter; send someone else

(Exodus 4:10). He continues on until God tells him okay. "What about your brother Aaron, he's a good speaker?" So, Moses made Aaron become his surrogate because Aaron had to speak to the seed. Surrogate mothers are used as a last resort for a woman who has tried every other alternative, yet nothing works. So, because nothing works, they decide to use another woman's body to conceive, carry the seed, and give birth. Many Christian women have surrogate mothers carrying them and their seeds. You are sitting and waiting for a prophetic word; stop waiting on someone else to give you a word, a prayer, and deliverance. Get your own breakthrough, you must produce, conceive, and give birth. Do not let your seed be REJECTED!!!

Chapter 5

<u>Fruitful but Denied:</u>

The Crab Fish mentality

Fruitful but Denied: The Crab Fish mentality

What does fruitful mean? When I had my son Elijah, I became pregnant again, shortly after. Although I was I was impregnated, I had a miscarriage. I was fruitful even though that seed was denied. Fruitfulness means that you can produce, but you are denied acknowledgement of your seed. Fruitfulness does not guarantee productivity.

Leah was fruitful yet denied.

The bible talks about Leah in Genesis 29:16. Leah's name means "wild cow" or gazelle. Leah was the oldest daughter of Laban and she was Jacob's wife. The bible speaks about Leah and how Jacob was working for his uncle. When Jacob arrives his uncle tells him, "Because we are relatives, you should work for me for free." Leah has pretty eyes, and she is the eldest daughter and it was customary for the eldest daughters to marry first, yet Jacob loved Rachel. She was beautiful, and the bible says that every part of her body was gorgeous; she had a lovely face and a body to die for. She looked like heaven to Jacob. Everyone that looked at the sister would notice Leah's eyes, yet they would become dazed when the saw Rachel. Jacob begins to have feelings and goes to tell Laban, "I'll work for you seven years if you give me Rachel to become my wife." Jacob, not know that he was being tricked, he worked seven years without pay for Rachel. I can see Jacob sweating and exhausted, but every time he saw Rachel, due to his love for her, it seemed like only a few days to him. When time came for the wedding night Laban tricked Jacob, it was very dark in the room, and Laban gave Jacob Leah instead of Rachel. Because it was too dark for him to see, Jacob did not notice, but when morning came, Jacob woke up to Leah. Jacob was mad and outraged; therefore, he had to wait seven more years to receive his blessing.

 Let's take a minute and look at Leah. I can imagine, she's feeling worthless, she feels that she was forced to marry, she feels unwanted and unloved. Since Leah was unloved the Lord blessed her womb and allowed her to produce a seed, while Rachel remained childless and barren. (Genesis 29: 32) Leah recognized that that the Lord saw her misery. Leah continued to give birth, hoping, wishing and praying that this time Jacob will surely love her because she was fruitful, but Leah was denied. Even though you are fruitful, you may not be full of the word.

Are you full of the anointing, yet you are still denied, why? There are people around you who are dream stealers. They will sit on you and pull on the anointing. They will try to tear you down by any means necessary. Sometimes you have to get away from your loved ones and your friends so you can come forth. The bible says that a prophet is not honored in his own country, it means that the hater that you will experience, are among you family, your friends, or maybe your prayer partner. No matter what Leah did or how many seeds she produced, she was still denied the love and affection from her husband. No matter how you are being used by God, there are some people who will never acknowledge that God's power works within you; they will never encourage you, and they will never get behind you and push you to go forward. Why, because of selfishness, jealousy and pride.

Hannah and Peninnah

Hannah's name means "gracious" and Peninnah's name means woman with rich hair, coral or pearl.

Peninnah had eight children by Elkanah, but Hannah did not. Each year Elkanah would give a special portion of sacrifice to Hannah, due to the fact that he loved her very much, even though she was barren. Peninnah at this time had been producing seeds and giving birth, but Elkanah did not love her as much as he loved Hannah. He would give Peninnah and her children a portion of sacrifice, but he gave Hannah a greater portion. I could see Peninnah saying "what does he want from me, I'm producing, I'm faithful, Hannah is barren, yet I am denied." Hannah begins to pray for a child.

Peninnah Acts Out

(I Samuel 1:6) We sometimes act like we don't understand when women act out; there are some people that cannot deal with hurt well. There are some people that cannot bottle up their emotions. There are some people who will never be able to act like nothing happened. So, yes through, hurts and pains Peninnah begins to act out. Peninnah begins make fun of Hannah, laughing at her, mocking her, because God had closed up her womb. She would taunt Hannah year after year. So, they went to the Tabernacle. It would be so bad that Hannah would break down crying. We must be careful not to allow our wounds and hurts to comeback in the form of revenge.

Crab Mentality

Crab mentality is used to describe a kind of selfish, shortsighted thinking, which means "If I can't have it, then you surely will not have it." This is when you are trying to go up the ladder, while other people try to pull you back down rather than letting you pursue your dream. They'll be a dream killer and stealer. This concept comes from an experiment. You can place crabs in a container, these crabs will be live and moving, but sometimes one of the crabs will try to escape, and if it looks like one of the crabs is going to experience freedom, the other crabs get together with one goal in mind, to pull it back down rather than to allow it to escape. They will join together against that one crab. Walking in this mentality, you have opened up your spirit and let jealousy walk in. In my ministry I have experienced "crab" mentality. We must expose this spirit. Where does this spirit come from? Jealousy!

Jealousy

Grace notes let us know:

What is jealousy? It is a mental attitude or emotional sin which is characterized by the resentment of another person's accomplishments, recognitions, or possessions; by hostility towards someone else who is believed to share the same advantage. Jealousy is a common result of the sin pride, or arrogance. Jealousy can be thought as a part of a collection of sins which begins with pride. A person filled with pride is blind to the grace of God. Pride makes a person think of himself as being on a pedestal that is far from reality and is greatly imagined. They think they have a real superiority to others. Jealousy is one of the strongest mental sins. Jealousy also comes from fear. People will become afraid if a friend is going to another level, and they will lose them. Jealousy destroys families and relationships. Jealousy embraces discord. Jealousy controls your emotions and your actions.

Dealing with Your Actions

Overcoming jealousy is so simple; you must first find the root of your jealousy. Second, you must admit you have jealousy. I remember when I received deliverance from jealousy. I loved spending time with my mom, and I was overprotective of her due to the fact that so many came into her ministry and used, abused, and destroyed her ministry. When she found a true friend, I could accept that this person was real. I was so jealous that if they would go out to eat, I would not go, and if they wanted me to ride, I refused to go. I played the blame game, not accepting that I was simply jealous, so I decided that I wanted to be healed. I went to this woman with tears flowing down my face and I told her that I'm jealous of you and that was the hardest thing to do. I had to admit that I was saved, speaking in tongue, and preaching, but I was jealous of my mother's friendship. She asked me why and I told her. She looked up at me and accepted my apology; she never brought that thing back up anymore. I still to this day see her and she's never brought it back up ever.

- ✓ <u>You must be satisfied with what you have</u>: learn how to be content

- ✓ Know that you will not be strong in every area.

- ✓ Trust God; fight where you're at

When you find yourself being denied while you are fruitful, you must understand that there are people and relationships that you feel like you can't live without. John Cena, the wrestler says, "You can't see me". He means that you can see me now, but you just see the shape I'm in now. You can't see my future; my time is now! It wasn't until I spoke that in my spirit that I started writing my book. Realize that your time is now! Make it happen; it will work, if you work it. Michael Jackson, before he died, had a project going on and he named it, "This is It".

I want you to know woman of God that this is it, you are in your last trimester and your water is about to break, the contractions are coming, and you're dilating. Yes, you may be denied, but you're fruitful. I cannot give up, I cannot lose my mind over haters, I can't lose my mind over men that I lost, I can't lose my mind over who doesn't like me, I can't lose my mind over being barren. So what if you're divorced, you still can't lose your mind, I can't lose my mind because I got a bad doctors report. I can't lose it because my husband cheated or because my children are disobedient. You are too close to your destiny and your dream; these things may cause you to feel denied, but you're fruitful. What does that mean? You are able to produce wealth, you have the ability to produce happiness, and you have the victory over bad experience all because God sees your fruitfulness.

Look at Joseph:

Joseph was the son of Jacob and Rachel. Joseph became the favorite son because God blessed them to have Joseph; not only in their old age, but at the time Rachel's womb was past child bearing. Joseph was given a coat of many colors, a coat that was fit for a king. Joseph's brothers got jealous because Joseph was destined for greatness.

I remember when I first told people that I wanted my own business. People laughed, got mad, and even jealous. My own family and friends started hating on me. People that I least expected to turn on me, did a "360."

Dream Stealers

You must remind yourself that you cannot always tell your dreams. You cannot expect everyone to pat you on the back and give you a honest "congratulations'" or a genuine hug. I've learned that I have to take my own hand and put it on my shoulder to encourage myself. Joseph shared his dream; his dream was that one day he would rule over his family, inspired by the envy of his brothers, they sold Joseph to a caravan of Israelites. (Gen. 37) In the end, the dream that Joseph had come true, you sometimes have to vision your dreams, be silent about what you see. Everything is not for everybody, and everyone doesn't need to know everything.

Artificial Insemination- this is a process by which sperm is placed into the reproductive tract of a female for the purpose of impregnating the female by using means other than sexual intercourse or "natural insemination."

Artificial Insemination Women

There are so many "A.I.W" (Artificial Insemination Women) these are women who never fast or pray before God, they are always running to different churches looking for a word. They have so many different words and doctrines (sperm cells in them) of many other religions on the inside of their spirit (womb), that they can't produce, because their barren, or have terminated new seeds.

Different Types of Births:

- Teen spiritual pregnancy- when God calls you at a young age, you're a carrier of the word at a young age, like when God used Mary.

- Twin spiritual Pregnancy- when God gives you more than one seed in the inside, when He allows you to appreciate more than one gift.

- <u>High Risk Spiritual Pregnancy</u>-when the enemy knows that you will be used by God and he knows that God has implanted on the inside of you, a dynamite seed, therefore you are "high risk." That means that the enemy will come against you at all costs. Why, because he knows that you are a threat to his kingdom. He knows that you have the power to bind and lose. So you are a high risk.

You may not be fruitful and you know, without a shadow of a doubt, that the seed is on the inside, but people are denying you. They are not congratulating, they're not cheering you on, or proud of your accomplishments. They're jealous, critical, negative, and doubtful. Thus know that what God has placed on the inside of you is fruitful, but he will never deny you. Men and women, haters and foes will deny or try to act like they don't see productivity, but you just keep producing. Yes I am fruitful and sometimes denied.

Chapter 6

<u>"Wrestling in the Womb" - A Forfeited Birthright</u>

"Wrestling in the Womb" - A Forfeited Birthright

A Wrestling in the Womb between Two Twin Brothers

Esau he was the eldest twin of Jacob, Isaac and Rebekah sons (Genesis 24:26). Esau was a favorite of his father; he also was hunter by trade. Isaac prayed to the Lord asking and pleading with God to let his wife become pregnant with twins. In her womb, the children struggled with each other. God told Rebekah, "Your sons are two rival nations. One nation will be stronger than the other." Esau was the first to come out of the two (Genesis 25:24). He was red at birth and so hairy that it looked like he was wearing clothes. The other twin came out gripping Esau's heel, so they named him Jacob.

Jacob's name was the Hebrew noun for "heel" or "he who cheats." As the boys grew up, Esau became a skillful hunter; he was a man who went out and got what he wanted, while Jacob was the kind of person who liked to stay at home with his parents. I'll say Jacob was comfortable. Their father, Isaac, loved Esau more due to the wild game he brought home, but Rebekah favored Jacob.

Forfeited Birthright

To forfeit something means that:

A) You gave it away

B) No one took it or stole it

C) You freely allow it to go away

D) Give up your rights by committing some offense or error.

If I could give an example of forfeit, I would use a wrestler.

A certain wrestler is the undefeated champion and no one has even come close to beating him yet. It's time for him to accept the challenge made by the challenger. He's the one everybody bought their ticket to see fight. He's the main attraction with the golden title. He has the fame, the prestige, the belt, the money, and all the glory; all the wrestlers want to be him and be in his shoes. Yet, when the match starts, he throws it and disappoints everyone by saying he's not going to defend himself, and by the way of forfeit, the challenger wins.

Greener Grass

I know we are not supposed to look at someone else's grass. I know that people say that they thought the grass was greener on the other side. However, if I can be truly honest with you, there are times when you're grass is dark brown and the sinner is living a better life than you. However, the Bible says that whatever's done for Christ will last.

What Made You Hungry?

Here Esau was, already with the favor of God resting on him. He comes in one day and says to his brother, "I'm starving". Esau was tired and exhausted from working all day. He asks his brother Jacob, "Give me some of the red stew you've made." Esau had everything he could've wanted, and he was at the point of getting everything he needed, but in the midst of his blessings, he got hungry. What were you hungering for? What caused your appetite for God to change? Did you get hungry for sin, doubt, addictions, and old habits? What did you have a craving for? There's some stuff in the will that God has left you.

<u>**The Will**</u>

You may feel like that you are going to always be in a place of dryness. You were misled about lots stuff. You have been overlooked, ignored, and conned out of what's rightfully yours; you must understand your inheritance left by God. He said in his word, "Beloved I wish above all things that you shall prosper even as your soul prospers." He left in his will (the Bible) for you to prosper. Our Father, and notice I said our Father, left us healing, deliverance, silver, gold, mansions, cars, the earth, and the fullest there of. It's in the will. Yes, then those statements we make, we will truly be walking in them:

1) The Head and Not the Tail

2) Royal Child

3) Above and Not Beneath

4) Lender and Not Borrower

5) First and Not the Last

6) Blessed and Highly Favored

Defense Attorney

I want to be your defense attorney. I want to represent you. The devil wants to challenge the will. Let's get your inheritance; let's get your stuff. Let me represent your case.

Birthright

A birthright consists of special privileges. If a man had two sons his estate would be divided into three portions. The eldest son would receive two portions and the youngest would receive the remainder.

Experience a Set-Up

There will be times in your life where people are going to try to set you up. They will try to overthrow and undermined you. Esau decided that he was so starved that he did not realize that he was getting ready for a set-up. I think that when you are blinded by starvation (the cares of the world), your judgment becomes off and therefore, things that you would automatically catch will get pass you because you are blinded by starvation. Jacob sees an opportunity to sell Esau's birthright. Jacob tells his brother, "I'll feed you, but you have to trade me your birthright." Esau, going on natural starvation, tells Jacob, "What good is a birthright to me, if I'm dead from starvation."

Just like Satan tried to tempt Jesus after he had fasted for forty days and nights, he was afterwards hungry. The Devil came and told Jesus, "If thou be the son of God, command that these stones be made bread." (Genesis 4:3-4). Jesus said unto Satan, "People need more than bread for their life; they must feed on every word of God."

Esau decides to swear an oath that he's going to give his brother all of his birthright. Esau sat down, and started eating bread and lentil stew. He's sitting there and enjoying the food, going on about his business; he wasn't even thinking about that he just gave away his birthright because he was hungry. Don't allow the enemy to cause hungriness to come upon you, and make you give in to starvation.

Embrace Your Traitor

What is a traitor? A traitor is person who betrays his country, a cause, or another's confidence.

Jacob Steals Esau's Blessings

(Genesis 27) It now came time for Isaac to speak blessings over Esau. Isaac at this point, was old and almost blind. He tells his son, any day now could be the day that I die; therefore, I need you to go out in the open country, and get me some wild game, prepare it just the way I like it. Season it good and bring it to me to eat. Then, I will pronounce the blessing that belongs to you, my first born son, before I die.

Embrace Your Traitor

Rebekah overheard Esau and his father's conversation. Now remember, Rebekah was both sons mother, and she should not have had greater love for one of her sons more than the other. She had a plan. Every person who schemes against you or plots against you, they already have a plan.

The Plan (Genesis 27:5)

She finds her son, Jacob, and tells him what she had overheard. She had the plan and she told him to do exactly what she says, "Go out to the flocks and bring me two fine goats. I'll prepare your father's favorite dish, then you will take it to your father, and he'll eat it and bless you instead of Esau." Jacob is confused, he begins to think about how Esau is hairy and how smooth his skin is. He's starts to get worried about what will happen if his father finds out that he's tried to trick him; instead of a blessing, he would get cursed. So, Jacob listened to his mother and followed her instructions. Rebekah cooked the food, gave it to Jacob, and put Esau's clothes on him; not only did she give him Esau's clothes, but his best clothes. She put a pair of gloves on him that she made from the skin of a hairy goat, and she took a strip of lamb skin and put it around his neck. She then gave him a meat dish, with rich aroma and some freshly baked bread. He carried the plate to his father, and he took the blessing. By the time Esau got back, he realized that his mother and younger brother plotted against him, and took his blessing.

 People will plot and plan against you, and trade on you for their own selfish reasons. Don't be mad at your haters or your traitors, embrace them. If I didn't have traitors and haters, I would have never pushed this hard. Sometimes you can say things without doing anything. So give your haters and traitors a hand clap.

Wrestle Until You Get It (Genesis 22-32)

Jacob got up during the night, and he decided to allow his two wives, two concubines and eleven sons to go across the Jabbock River. This left him alone in the camp, and a man came and wrestled with Jacob until dawn. When the saw that he couldn't win the match, he struck Jacob's hip, and knocked it out of socket.

The man says, "Let me go, for its dawn." But Jacob says to the man, "I will not let you go unless you bless me." Sometimes you have to make your blessing come, you must be willing to do whatever it takes to get what rightfully belongs to you. Don't let go, even if you have to wrestle, pull, tug, or slide. Never let go until you get your blessing. Don't forfeit your birthright. Everything that God promised you, it's getting ready, woman of God, to happen. Don't throw your seed to someone else because you are getting ready to produce. You are ready to give birth.

Chapter 7

It's Delivery Time

Push your seed and give Birth

It's Delivery Time: Push your seed and give Birth

To deliver means to:

Spiritually;

1. Come through for some reason or person

2. Present something

3. Get you out of something

4. Make good or a promise or vow

Naturally;

1. To allow the seed which you have carried for nine months that to be produced

Delivery

You may feel like you've been in this situation a long time and it looks like all the odds are stacked against you. Poverty and lack are haunting and hounding you. Sickness is following you. Your mind is confused, because you're tired of waiting; your body is weary and exhausted. Your spirit is broken and vexed. Your soul is restless and uneasy. Your eyes are swollen from crying all night long. Your voice is hoarse, shaking and trembling as you keep crying out to God to deliver you. I wrote this book to let you know that today God will deliver. It does not matter what obstacles you are facing; God will deliver.

The first thing you must realize is who you are, we sometimes have identity crises, or memory loss and we forget who our father is and what he has promised you. Do you believe that our daddy sees what you are going through and he is going to continue to move his face in the other direction? No, God is not like that, he will deliver and delivery is now. You have to let go of every blockage or stronghold that attacks you today, deliverance is now. You've got to break the curse. Satan has had you hostage in your mind for too long, he has robbed, raped, stripped and chained your strength.

You can't see me but my time is now

It's time to get in, it's time to fight it's time to put your legs in the stir ups and push your seed out, yes you may sweat a little, you'll feel the pain, but keep pushing.

Delivery Time

As we were rolling me in the wheelchair to the labor room, all I could think is after all this time, I'm getting ready to hold my seed.

Get Dressed

The first thing they tell you to do is get undress, you first have to put the proper garments on. Why do they tell you to take off your regular clothes and put on the hospital gown? To deliver there are certain things that you must have or not have on, when you are getting ready to deliver naturally and spiritually; so you must dress yourself.

Ephesians 6:10

- Breastplate – a piece of elaborate embroidery about nine inches square worn by a high priest upon his breasts. The purpose of the breastplate was to show the glory and beauty of the Lord, as a means of making a decision, and to be a continuing memorial before the Lord.

- Belt of truth- that which is reliable and can be trusted. You must dress yourself with truth. The Bible lets us know that God hates lying tongues. All liars will have their part in the lake of fire.

<u>Feet shod with the preparation of the gospel peace.</u>

The sense of being well, and fulfillment that comes from God and is dependent on his presence. You need peace in your life. God does not want you stressed and worried the peace of God needs to rain in your heart, mind, spirit and soul. There was a little song that says, "Don't worry, be happy." So when worry comes, you must not allow worry to make you stressed. Stress and worry brings about heart trouble, strokes, high blood pressure, cancer and all kinds of sickness. So allow the Lord to grant you peace

- <u>The Shield of Faith</u>: Simply is believing what you cannot see. Faith is, according to Hebrews 11:1, the substance of things hoped for, the evidence of things not seen. What that means is that faith is the assurance that we hope for is going to happen. You need the shield of faith to stop the enemy's fiery arrows.

- <u>The Helmet of Salvation</u>: What is salvation? Salvation simply means being set apart. You need the salvation of the Lord. Salvation is simply giving up old ways and habits and trading them for the new. Sin stinks in God's nostrils. The Lord says "I wish that you were neither hot nor cold, because you are lukewarm, I will spit you out of my mouth".

Salvation is a lifestyle; I love being "saved". I love having a relationship with the Lord. If you have been searching for something and you just don't know what it is, if you have not given your life to the Lord, this is the right time and moment. Why don't you allow the Lord to come into your life?

Repeat after me:

<u>Sinner's Prayer</u>

Lord I know that I have sinned against you, I am truly sorry. Please forgive me Lord. I ask you to wash me and cleanse me. Lord, I want to turn me from my evil ways. I invite you in my life and my heart; Lord this day I give myself to you, thank you for your forgiveness and your salvation. If you prayed that prayer, Hallelujah you're saved. Welcome to the family.

So you have your gown and all of a sudden contractions start...

<u>Contractions</u>

What are contractions? The process of becoming smaller, it's also the process in which a muscle becomes or is made shorter and tighter.

Labor Contractions

During birth, contractions are when the abdomen becomes hard. Between the contractions, the uterus relaxes and the abdomen becomes soft. Contractions move in a wave, like motions from top to bottom.

Spiritual Contractions

These are nothing more than trials and tribulations. What are trials? Trials are the act of being tested, tried, or putting to proof; that is a state of pain or anguish. Trails sometimes make you feel like they came to destroy you or pull you down, but trails come to make you strong. Trails come so that you may have;

1. First, Strength-God knows how much you can handle. Life will not put more on you than you can bear. Therefore, you must understand the trials come to allow you to know that you can make it. You may have to go through, with tears running down your face, but when you come through that storm, you will then realize that you are stronger than you were before.

2. Secondly, trails come to settle you. This means that it will place you or appoint you to your rightful place. When you are a Christian you need to be settled. You need one place

to call your worship home. There are so many church jumpers, every time something small happens you end up leaving and you have become like a helpless baby, still wanting the, bottle, the nipple and the breast. You have to learn to bloom where you are planted. Allow God to plant you (settle) you in the place that he has for you.

3. Thirdly, trails come to establish you, which means, trials come to set you up; trials come to build you to a firm and stable place. Trials do not come to make you unstable but they come to establish you; to let you know where you are headed, to put you in the right place so you can receive the true blessings of God.

4. The fourth reason trials come are, because God wants you Perfect, which means God wants you to be complete and whole. So many times we feel like we cannot be made whole, but think about the woman who had the issue of blood. Just for a minute let's talk about her. She was bleeding, she was broken, she was wounded, but she realized that if she could just touch the hem of his garment, she will be made whole. All God wants to do is make you whole. So, go ahead and go through the trials, the tests and the contractions of life, but when you finish going through, just look at your seed.

I'm reminded about how I put the hospital gowns on and how I started feeling the pains and how it was uncomfortable, but I wanted my seed. You've got to press past your contractions of life, so what if you were lied on. So what if you are talked about, mistreated, or misunderstood, baby, it's just a contraction, pushing out your seed; Come on and push!

So, I experienced the contraction but I could not push yet due to the fact that my water had not broken.

The Breaking of the Water

In a natural delivery, the water breaking is the sign that the sac holding the amniotic fluid has broken. This fluid is the protection of the baby. It protects the baby from infection and bumps to the mother's belly. This fluid protects the baby from being exposed. Isn't it a blessing when your water breaks?

Spiritual Water Breaking

This is when God is saying, okay, I have allowed you to break loose. When I felt that you were not ready before, but I feel that you are ready now. So, I'm going to allow the stuff that has been holding you back, to become broken. So therefore, he has caused you to break, so that you may be able to break free. So your water has broken, which means that it's time to push.

What happens after your water breaks? You are getting ready to push out your seed.

Timing is important.

In the natural child birthing, if your water breaks and you do not push soon, you are exposed to infection. When God allows you to break free, timing is very important, you can't continue to wait, and cause problems in your delivery. You've broken free from all those bondages of the enemy. The liquid is pouring and gushing out. The womb is being cleansed. It's time to push. This is the moment you have been waiting on. Although labor may not start immediately after your water breaks, delivery of your seed is near.

Now It's Delivery Time:

After you've been through the swollen feet, the morning sickness, the vomiting, the undesirable taste buds, all those doctor visits, now it's time to push.

Push:

It's time to push; God has given you this seed, now you are going to push to produce or are you going to ignore your seed? The pushing stage occurs after the cervix is completely dilated and no longer in front of the baby's head. A smooth passageway now exits through in which you can push your seed from the uterus and down through the birth canal.

A Support Person

Maybe you're a little frightened because you feel like you're all alone. Maybe you went through delivery before and it did not come forth; even though labor failed you before, I want you to know that I have been assigned to be your support person and I will not leave you until you push your seed Woman of God, people are waiting on you. You have been through hell and storms and it has caused you to feel as if you're not ready, but right now I've got your hand. Right now you can lean on me; I want you to push past all the hurts and the pain. I know people said, "you would never amount to anything." I know your struggle, but you've got to push! Your heart has been broken, your feelings have been hurt, you've been misunderstood, and your friends have turned out to be your enemies. You found out your loved ones really didn't have your back because they were jealous, but this day, you begin to push. Life will be greater than you have ever experienced before. I had to push past haters. I had to push past gossipers and liars. I had to push past poverty, lack, envy, and strife. Baby it's time to push, come on, grab my hand, let's push together, let's bring this seed forth together.

Get in Position

You must get ready to get yourself if position. Sometimes you're pushing, but you're not in position. You have to get yourself up to produce your seed. It may take you crying, exercising, it may take forgiveness, but whatever it takes, you must push!

It's Time to Breathe

Air coming into or out of your mouth or body is breathing. The breathing technique used for pushing depends on what works for you. Grunting and groaning is a form of breathing, it also helps while you are pushing. Allow yourself freedom to make sounds that comes naturally. Breathing helps you to relax. It's time to breathe; you have to exhale the entire negative that people place on you during your pregnancy. Push and breathe, now push harder than you have ever pushed before and watch your seed come forth.

God could have chosen someone else to impregnate; he could have allowed you to be spiritually barren, but he did not, he placed the seed in your womb, therefore you must give birth. It's time to stop making excuses and

PUSH YOUR SEED:

Pregnant with a Seed: Lord Please Help me to Deliver

This book was truly inspired by the Lord. Out of all of the times I struggled with pushing into my destiny, I never dreamed God would allow me to write about it. Lady Georgetta Ward was born in Memphis, Tennessee. She is the Co Pastor & First Lady of the Pure Harvest International Church, under the leadership of her husband, Bishop Ralph Ward III. She is a woman of vision and is truly anointed by God. God has inspired her to push other women to deliver their seeds.